Coyote
on the
Bridge

Coyote
on the
Bridge

A Healing Journey

~

Susan Woodward

~ ALDER CREEK PRESS ~

Coyote on the Bridge
A Healing Journey

Copyright © 2025 by Susan Woodward

Published by Alder Creek Press, Truckee, California.

MEMOIR / GRIEVING / HEALING / NATURE / HIKING

Coyote on the Bridge is a memoir about the unexpected death of my husband after forty years of marriage and how I turned to solo hiking for healing. This work is based on my memories, journals and conversations with family and friends.

Print ISBN: 979-8-9903960-0-5

Printed in the United States of America.

Cover and interior design by Gilman Design, Larkspur, California.

Photo credits:
Cover: *Coyote on the Bridge*, Susan Woodward
Cover Back: photos, James R. Woodward
Page 30: *Early Years Backpacking*, James R. Woodward
Page 32: *Three Generations*, Judi Woodward Archbold
All other photos from Woodward family archives

For Alex, James and Drew

CONTENTS

Prologue: What Trail is This?   vii

I. A LIFE INTERRUPTED

A Knock on the Door   1

II. THE TRAILHEAD

First Date   12
Running Interference   15
View from the Endzone   24

III. SNAGS

The First Goodbye   33
Day-to-Day   39
Scanning the Ridgeline   42
I Should Have Known   47
The Last Three Miles   54

IV. RETURN TO THE MOUNTAINS

The Christmas Stocking   60
Coyote on the Bridge   62
Return to the Mountains   66
Crossing   69
The Scout   77

Epilogue: Gathering Up a Child   81
Acknowledgements   85
Author's Note   87
About the Author   89

Prologue: What Trail is This?

KNEELING ON THE FLOOR, I dug through the box of US Geological Survey maps one more time. The maps, all tossed into the box one on top of the other, were left folded to display a quadrant of our backpacking hikes rather than being folded back the way they were purchased. The map of our most recent hike, the Bear Valley trail out to Arch Rock in the Point Reyes National Seashore, was askew on top of the pile. Anxious about where I was headed, I could not find the right map. Annoyed, I shoved the box back into the closet, quickly turned and headed out without a map.

I arrived at the Alder Creek trailhead, close to our cabin in Truckee. I lifted the hatch. I had brought the wrong pack. This one was too heavy for me to shoulder easily. In the throes of grief and not knowing what I would need, I had over-packed. Normally Chris would have helped me lift the pack out of the car and swing it up onto my back. Now I must shift the pack to a nearby rock, where it balanced precariously until I looped my arms through the straps. Stabilized, I heaved the pack up and settled the weight on my hips. I leaned forward, pulled down to shorten the shoulder straps and then cinched the waist belt.

I stood up. I took a moment to feel centered, the heaviness of loss compressing my height. I took a deep breath. I couldn't procrastinate any longer. I needed this hike to learn if I could still do this. Grabbing my poles, I lowered the hatch, locked the car, and turned towards the trail. The first part of the trail was well traveled and familiar. But looking ahead the path disappeared into a stand of pines where I would be making my way alone.

I took the first step.

I. A LIFE INTERRUPTED

A Knock on the Door

I T WAS EARLY, JUST an ordinary Tuesday morning. The green light on the clock illuminated the time, 4:30 a.m. There was a stirring in bed, covers tossed aside, lights flicked on. We both rose, the cat jumped off the bed and beat us downstairs.

Chris dressed quickly—jeans, loafers, a white shirt, blue blazer—the travel outfit he didn't have to think about. A toothbrush got thrown into his toilet kit, the kit zippered into the top of his carry-on bag. He had his routine down. Still in my sweatpants and tee shirt, I followed him down the stairs. I insisted on a proper goodbye hug and kiss at the front door, even though he would only be gone four days on this trip. The routine was familiar to both of us.

"I'll text you later when I arrive," he said as he turned away and headed into the garage.

"Safe travels."

The itinerary for this East Coast trip was routine for him. Drive to SFO, board the 7:00 a.m. United flight to JFK, pick up a rental car. He was scheduled to attend a board meeting the next day. A routine trip he made quarterly, like the hundreds of business trips he had taken over forty years of married life. I climbed back up the stairs to try and get another hour of sleep in before my workday started. The cat followed me and resettled in his warm indentation on the comforter. I went back to sleep.

The days passed routinely. Whenever Chris traveled, he left me a voicemail at work after his morning run, chiding me for not being in the office yet. The time change always seemed to work to his advantage for these messages. Not always remembering what time zone he was in, sometimes his voicemail would startle me before I settled into my own workday. While he would often use humor to tease me about being "late" to the office, I could hear the caring in his voice. He was an old-fashioned guy and didn't want to show concern about these frequent work separations. He was not one to show his emotions very often.

On Thursday I arrived home at noon, changed into jeans and a well-worn plaid shirt. My carry-on was already packed and stood by the table in the kitchen. I leaned over my desk and wrote a note for the cat sitter. I was heading down to Southern California for the weekend to see my dad.

My phone vibrated. A text popped up from one of Chris's best friends from college, the one whose company board meeting Chris had gone East to attend. "Call me" it read, very unusual. Then I remembered I hadn't heard from Chris that morning.

I called back and Rob picked up immediately.

He skipped a greeting and started talking, "Things don't look good here, Woody is not answering his phone and we can't find him."

I didn't understand what he was saying. "What do you mean you can't find him?"

My thoughts started spinning. How do you lose someone who is 6'3", a tall guy with white hair and an infectious smile? "I'm leaving for the airport in a few minutes, I'm supposed to be going down to see my dad this weekend."

"You can't leave the house now." His words hung in the air.

Details started to come out. "Chris is not in his room, the cleaning service wanted to go in and clean, and the inn had to call the police to be let into his room. His phone is there in the room, but his rental car is not in the lot and his wallet and keys are missing. He must be out in his jogging clothes. I'll call you when I learn more. The police are here."

We hung up. I was stunned and so far away. "The police are here" reverberated in my brain. What was going on? I started to feel a pit in my stomach.

I called the airline to cancel my flight, but I couldn't get through to customer service. I hung up and sat down at my desk. I phoned my dad. He thought I had arrived early in Southern California and needed a ride from the airport.

"No, Dad, I can't come right now. Something's not right; they can't find Chris and he hasn't checked out of his motel room. He's supposed to be driving to New York today for another board meeting tomorrow."

My dad paused and let this information sink in. His silence made me nervous. He had always been good at figuring things out. His silence on the line continued. I felt panicky.

"Dad? Dad?"

Finally, he responded, "Okay, stay there and let me know when you know something."

"Okay."

We hung up.

IN THE MEANTIME, A refuse truck driver in Avon had driven twice past a car pulled over on one of the thoroughfares on his regular route. The car's driver looked like he was checking his phone. But the third time the truck driver went past, he noticed the man hadn't moved at all, and he called the police.

———

Rob called again. "Sue, the worst has happened. Wood has passed away."

The police had arrived at the location and found my husband slumped forward in the rental car, a scene they label in the police report as "an untimely death. No trauma was noted, there was no alcohol or drugs in the vehicle. Mr. Woodward's wallet was present, left on the back seat of his rental vehicle."

———

Time was suspended. I couldn't think what I should do next. I couldn't do anything but sit there at the kitchen table and gasp for air. I put my head on my crossed arms on the table and started to cry. In the middle of summer, I shivered. Momentarily paralyzed. Across the country a police investigation began. It would take two months to conclude.

Finally, I stood up. I took a few steps over to the kitchen island, leaned against the counter for support. My life as a widow was supposed to start years, decades, from now. Chris's sudden death was not in the plan. Instead, our plan involved my early retirement, some sort of volunteer or part-time public service endeavor, a rental house in New Zealand's South Island for a month, hiking trips, maybe a son's marriage. He would grin sheepishly when I confided my fingers were crossed for a grandbaby. We had milestones to look forward to, to celebrate and share together.

———

How could this have happened? He seemed so healthy, he jogged or swam every day, he ate lots of salads and had no history of chronic health problems. He had started medication for borderline high cholesterol only two weeks ago. I had just talked with him yesterday; we made plans for Sunday night, and he had looked forward to getting home. His youthful enthusiasm and zest for life infused our sons' and my lives, from everyday routine chores to special holidays and celebrations. Now he was gone. I couldn't get my brain around this. I was numb. I started to shake. I sat down at the kitchen table again, laid my head on my crossed arms, and started to cry. Not just sniffling little tears; I started to heave, shake, sob. I thought I was going to throw up but I couldn't remember eating anything since breakfast.

Time passed. I had no idea how much time, but my breathing started to become steadier. At that moment, I'm not sure if I had any more tears left.

I tried to think and compose myself. Okay, be strong for the kids; you've got to pull it together. I started giving myself pep talks. You can get through this, you are stronger than you know, you were the only gal who could keep up with him: the hiking, the skiing, the single parenting when he traveled. You can do this. I just couldn't think what this was.

I had no sense of how to prioritize anything or whom to call first. The silence of Chris's absence was deafening, and this was just the beginning. I started to be afraid of being alone and of not knowing what to expect next. I was a planner. This was not the plan. So instead, I went and fed the cat.

My dreams had shattered. Instead of heading to Idaho next month to test our empty nest compatibility before retiring, I would be alone now, without a map or a guide to follow. Thrown into circumstances beyond my control, I envisioned bushwhacking my way through the overwhelming grief and shock that accompanied my sudden loss.

I imagined hacking away at obstacles along this unexpected new path, as I pushed through bushes, branches and climbed over rocks in the way. Faced with an uncertain future, I had to literally bushwhack to create a new way to live alone. Normally, I would have reached behind my daypack and found my compass clipped to an outside loop, a trusted tool for hikers to orient themselves to the path they want to follow. But my compass was broken; the red needle refused to orient towards north and it kept jiggling around, even while I tried to hold it level and steady. My hand kept shaking. With a broken compass and without Chris by my side, I started to realize how lost I was.

But the first thing I had to do was call my dad.

We planned to call each of my sons and convene at the family home over the next few days. I wrote down his flight number and arrival time in my moleskin. My hand was shaky. I didn't trust my memory and I started to write everything down.

Dad's plan was fly up on Saturday with our youngest son, Drew. Over the next week, we would be comforted by Pops' presence. He planned to spend three weeks with me. A 10th Mountain Division infantryman in World War II and a hands-on dad and grandpa, he earned the affectionate name "Pops" when his first-born grandson learned to talk. Over time, he would become our support system, guide, counselor, and chief comforter. He was close to our sons and their partners.

That evening, James, our middle son, arrived home from work early. It was Thursday. We collapsed in each other's embraces, and I could barely get the words out. He was in shock, and we tried to talk through what must have happened, but it didn't make sense to us. Slowly, he climbed the stairs and retreated to his room.

I sat down at my desk in the kitchen and called Chris's brother, Rick. He was shocked. The news of his older brother's death was shocking to all of us, but it was especially hard on those closest to him. He said he would call his sister and cousin.

"Yes, that would be really helpful, and I will share more

details with you as I learn them," I replied.

We agreed to no social media postings. I did not want our oldest son and daughter-in-law to learn of Chris's death as they passed through an airport the next day, returning from a babymoon trip. Another moment passed and I started to be afraid again. I began to realize I was going to have to be the head of my family now.

A knocking at the door interrupted my calls, and I kept crying. The knocking started again. Someone rang the doorbell. I didn't like answering the door at night by myself when Chris was traveling. I tried to compose myself and walked to the front door. Breathe. I unlocked the deadbolt, opened the door, and faced two county sheriffs. Men in blue uniforms with guns and badges but no hats on. One held a clipboard.

"Hi," I could barely speak. My voice isn't a very strong voice anyway, but it was a quaky voice of fear that night.

"Hello," the taller of the two started to speak. "We are here from the Alameda County Sheriff's office. Are you Susan Woodward?"

"Yes," I nodded.

"Do you know why we are here?"

I hesitated. Rob had alerted me, concerned I would be alone, that the sheriffs might arrive at our house that night. I should be prepared for this notification of Chris's death.

"Yes. Do you want to come in?"

They stepped forward and followed me into the kitchen. They looked around. This house was built in an old California mission style with Saltillo tile floors, wrought iron hardware, wooden windows, high ceilings, and a Spanish tile backsplash in the kitchen. The walls were hand stuccoed. Chris and I had built this home after we lost our former home in the Oakland firestorm of 1991.

The officers and I stood at the kitchen island. The one with the clipboard set it down on the island countertop and turned to face me.

"Do you want a glass of water or something?" I asked him.

"No. We're here to inform you of the death of your husband, Christopher Woodward. He died earlier today in Avon, CT. We are in touch with the police department there, and it is our duty as Alameda County sheriffs to notify next of kin."

The word "kin" slapped me. Internally I raged. No, I am his wife; we were college sweethearts, friends, lovers, spouses, parents, each other's sounding boards, best friends. Now I'm a "next of kin"?

"Okay." I tried to keep breathing. This was too much to process. Couldn't they just go away? "Is there something I need to sign?"

"No." They both turned simultaneously, as though they had choreographed delivering this message before.

"Okay, do you leave any kind of form or something?"

They hesitated. "No, we don't leave any forms. Is there someone here with you?" The tone of the taller sheriff's voice changed; I'm not sure this was part of their script.

"Yes. One of our sons is upstairs."

"Then we will leave now." I walked slightly ahead of them and reopened the front door.

Somehow, I managed to choke some words out: "Thank you for doing your job." They walked away, through the court-yard and up the brick steps to their patrol car parked along the curb.

Closing the door, I turned and slid my back down along its redwood grooves, knees bent in a vee until I squatted on my haunches. I began to cry again.

As the sheriffs left, I realized I forgot to cancel my flight to Southern California. I decided to deal with that tomorrow as I also needed to plan to fly East in the next few days.

I began the task of calling some of our best friends, phone numbers I recalled without looking them up. The news was horrible. I could hardly speak on the phone, but those closest to Chris and to us as a couple got the news firsthand.

One friend was in such shock, he commented that he is the one who is overweight and drinks too much red wine, that it should have been him who died. My best friend from high school started crying and I realized she thought my dad had died…I talked louder into the mobile: "No, no, it's not Pops, it's Chris who died." Standing outside on the deck for better cell service, I got a chill. Those words just hung in the air.

It was the first time I said it; my husband died before my own father.

I recalled all those times, standing in the kitchen, grieving in advance for the eventual loss of my Pops, a concern I had whenever he fell ill. Chris would wrap me up in a bear hug and always say, "Yes, it will be awful when Pops dies, but I will take care of you and help you get through it." I was still in shock when I thought of this, how it all got turned around. Now my father would be the one to support the boys' partners, the boys and me as we grieved the loss of their father and my husband.

I tried to sleep that night, but it felt awkward to be in the big bed. I started to realize that his side of the bed was always going to stay made from here on out. The cat jumped up on the bed and began circling around Chris's side, sniffing, and gently pawing at his pillow. After circling, he finally settled down, green eyes blinking at me as I tried to go to sleep.

On Friday morning, I started to get text updates from the parents of our daughter-in-law. They were picking the kids up at SFO and would tell them to come to my house, our family home, as soon as possible. I looked down and realized I was still in my jeans and plaid shirt, my airplane clothes from yesterday. Did I sleep in these clothes? In a haze I couldn't remember showering, so I guess I did. I went upstairs to brush my teeth.

Using his own key, our oldest son Alex rushed into the house and when he saw me standing alone in the kitchen, unable to hide my sorrow, he knew, before I could say anything, that something was wrong. I started to tell him of his father's death, but my words choked me. My daughter-in-law Elana joined our hug circle; all we could do was hang on to each other and cry.

The days slipped by as disbelief set in. Awaking on Saturday, I wondered what day it was. I reminded myself to pick up my dad and Drew. Despite the security at the airport, the three or us clung to each other for too long at the curb before I helped Pops step up into the Xterra. We arrived home.

Our three sons, their partners and my dad were now home, each in various rooms throughout the house. We began to share stories with each other, supporting each other, and knew that by staying strong for each other, we would get through this initial stage of shock and deep sadness.

The rest of that day was a blur, with us making and receiving phone calls. More of our family arrived. Chris's brother and his wife arrived with food, flowers, and a card. They knew Pops from their own visits to Southern California. We shared feelings and thoughts. Their presence comforted us. I was relieved to have family around me to help with the calls and messages. I resumed making other calls, mostly to extended family members. I went back upstairs to cancel my Southern California flights and rebooked flights to the East Coast for the next day.

I could hardly think. Flowers and food started to arrive; the kids became adults and took over. They were serving food, cleaning up, intercepting phone calls, making lists, hosting friends, going on walks to rest and take a break from the shared grief.

Despite offers from family members to accompany me to the East Coast to claim his body, I experienced an overwhelming sense that I had to do this task alone. Whether it was my penance for not being there when Chris died, I didn't know. I only knew that it was my responsibility, and I was unable to share it with anyone else.

I left on Sunday morning for the East Coast and could only focus on bringing Chris home.

II. THE TRAILHEAD

First Date

As a seventeen-year-old high school senior, I waited with my parents in the front room of our home for my date. My long, blue empire style dress with an embroidered flower across the bust and white Bernardo sandals was a popular look in beach communities in Southern California. Mom's borrowed red shawl was draped over my shoulders. The living room was furnished in a comfortable 1970s way with gold pile carpeting and some antiques, a brown flowered couch, and two gold plush chairs with carved arms angled towards the front door. Mom, an elementary school teacher, and Dad, a city administrator, were proud to have been able to move into this newly built tract home in 1964. There was a separate bedroom for each child. A lot of thought had gone into choosing the carpet.

Outside, a twenty-one-year-old senior at the University of California, Berkeley pulled up to the curb in his '67 Ford Fairlane and honked the horn. My parents startled and looked at each other. I started to head for the front door.

"No. You wait here until he comes to the door," my dad instructed.

I cringed. What if he didn't like my parents, or they didn't like him, or worse, what if he didn't come to the door? My stomach was in a knot, my jaw clenched.

After a minute or two he opened the driver-side door and unwound his tall frame out of the car. He straightened out the angles of his knees and elbows, pulled his shoulders back, patted down his brown hair flopping over his collar, and headed for our front door. I watched his approach through the lace curtains. Plaid pants, a blue sailboat print button-down, a red and blue striped tie, and a navy blazer completed his frat boy look as he stepped up to the porch. Instead of trying the doorbell, he knocked on the door.

Mom opened the door, cautiously at first. He ducked his head sideways and stepped inside. His height dwarfed my mom and a slight awkwardness occurred as greetings went around the room. Dad turned towards him, twisted his neck to look up and smiled. I sensed Dad wanted to like him. I introduced him and reminded my parents he was my high school tennis friend's brother, home from college. His name was Chris. It was his great smile that put us all at ease.

My parents had a brief conversation with us—we were headed off to the Chart House for dinner and would be returning right after. I was getting nervous, not about going out with him but about getting carded. I'd heard college boys liked to drink and my fake ID wasn't that good. I was anxious, but excited too. We started to leave the house, but Mom stopped us.

"Here, just let me get a picture," she asked.

We glanced at each other, and I raised my eyebrows a tiny bit as if to say, "Please stay, this will only take a minute." We obligingly stood in front of the brick fireplace. I stepped up on the hearth to appear two inches taller. He gently put his arm around my shoulder; we both smiled at the camera.

Chris assured my folks we would be back soon after dinner. Their anxiety, as their high school daughter headed out on a date with a college man, eased a bit. They smiled and waved as we left the house. I expected them to wait up in the family room for our return.

We walked down the sidewalk lined with Mom's favorite Shasta daisies. He was already circling behind the car, getting in over on the driver's side. It took me a second to realize he wasn't going to open the door for me, so I opened it myself and got in, and reached for the seat belt. It was only then that I realized he had left the engine running.

Running Interference

WE HEADED SOUTH ON Highway 101 on a Friday afternoon in my boyfriend's Ford Fairlane. The blue vinyl seats were warm despite the open windows. The Memorial Day weekend was always spent at his grandparent's ranch in Malibu Canyon, a strong tradition. Loaded up with sleeping bags, pillows, tennis racquets, swimsuits, provisions for a breakfast for twenty-four ranch guests and a case of beer, we ditched our Friday classes at Berkeley to get a head start on the weekend. If you were a friend who could play tennis, mah jongg, or bridge, you were likely to earn an invite to this family reunion.

Ever since Chris could remember, his brother, sister and cousin had spent Memorial Day at the ranch, and sometimes even a whole summer as well. The ranch meant not only hiking and riding horses, playing tennis and swimming, but also doing chores with Aunt Barbara. Mucking out the stalls, priming the water pump, and doing the dishes were routine assignments.

Chris and I had been friends, introduced by his sister, Judi. We met after eighth grade in local summer tennis clinics and again as freshmen in our high school's Girls Athletic Association sports program. We played volleyball and basketball in the fall and winter, softball, and tennis in the spring. In our junior year, we began playing doubles with her brother and his best friend, both college juniors and both named Chris. They would be home for spring breaks and summers. Sometimes we played mixed doubles, rotating partners and sometimes we played gals against the guys. On a rare occasion, we beat them, much to their chagrin.

Over years of tennis, bowling, going to the beach and an occasional movie, Chris and I became a dating couple, especially after I transferred to Berkeley in my junior year. By then he was in graduate school and worked as a bartender. I was studying sociology, competed on the women's tennis team and worked at a local pro shop. Even with school and work, Saturday afternoons in the fall found us at his fraternity house for a beer or two before walking up to the stadium for the football game. This was my first Memorial Day weekend at the ranch, and I was nervous, but excited, too.

We cruised down Highway 101, through Salinas and Soledad. We passed The Correctional Training Facility and continued through San Luis Obispo. Songs by the Eagles and America played on the radio and as we neared the coastline, a refreshing blast of fog-cooled air hit us. We continued south, where we passed the Sea Shanty with its billboard "Cold Steaks and Warm Beers". Chris always insisted on being the driver and never wanted a break. I was content to ride shotgun, often reading a book or just listening to the radio. I gave ample notice when I needed a pit stop, as he would kiddingly begrudge me any time lost on the road.

Looking back, even then I sensed he was going to be his own person, on his own life path. Trying to convince him to stop for a bathroom break may have been an inkling of what lay ahead, but I was too enamored with his good looks, positive outlook, and charismatic smile to even notice his strong independent streak. He might start a day with a hike on a trail, but usually by noon, he wanted to deviate from the path well-worn by others. An incredible map reader, he would want to forge a new path, bushwhacking through the brush to save time and arrive at a pass where the view would be even more incredible than if we had stayed on the trail. I would learn this about him over the following summers. At that moment on our first road trip, I was just happy to be near him and on our way to the ranch.

Our conversations in the car were often brief, covering who we thought would be arriving ahead of us, if a certain cousin had a new boyfriend or girlfriend, and if a certain guest had figured out how to serve a tennis ball yet. We speculated over the tennis draw and laughed nervously if Aunt Barbara would be our tennis partner in the first round. We were a competitive bunch after all, and winning the tournament meant a whole year of family bragging rights. The winner's name was imprinted on a Dymo label maker and placed on the base of the trophy—a metal Wilson tennis ball can with the wings of victory screwed onto the top of the can. Chris was often the instigator at family events and had created the trophy that would be awarded in the years that followed at the ranch.

We drove past Isla Vista, where my parents met at UC Santa Barbara. We passed surfers' heaven, the Rincon, where they spent many a Saturday morning with a thermos full of coffee, watching the surfers shoot the curl. Chris's folks were Berkeley grads; their college reminiscences were of Big Games against Stanford and their friends whose college experience was interrupted by World War II. We recalled these parental stories and suspected a few of them would be rehashed over the weekend.

Past Ventura, we finally reached the exit, Kanan Road. We headed west towards the Pacific Ocean. We drove another few miles and entered the tunnel where someone had painted "The Pink Lady" in all her splendor. Finally, we arrived at the turnoff to the ranch. The first part of the road was pavement, then a long dirt road to the heart of the property. The rusty gate had been propped open as Aunt Barbara was expecting a crowd this Memorial Day. Our windows were rolled down and the dryness of the air hit our faces. There was very little humidity in the canyon in late May and the air was tinged with the smell of coastal oaks and manzanita.

Slowly, we drove past the tennis court with its original 1927 surface. Chris's stories of ranch lore filled me with excitement, but some trepidation. Many a family argument had occurred over whether to play a "let" due to some quirk of the court surface that had resulted in the infamous "ranch bounce." We inched along slowly over the wooden plank bridge to not stir up too much dust and continued up towards the white clapboard farmhouse. The dogs on the back porch had already stirred. Chris honked the horn upon our arrival which added decibels to their barking refrains. In the early dusk, lights flicked on outside and family members and friends began to file out the screen door. It slammed multiple times. The Oakley sisters competed in shrill voices:

"You made good time. What time did you leave?"

"How long did it take? You didn't leave before noon, did you?"

"You're here early. We didn't expect you for another hour or so."

"Hey, where do you want this stuff?"

Many hands reached into the back of Chris's car and in an instant, it was unloaded. One of the teenagers, yet to get his driver's license, jumped in behind the wheel and moved the car to the dirt lot up by the pool. There it remained for the next few days, the vinyl interior baking in the hot sun.

Our arrival was one of many that night. Siblings and parents from Southern California, aunts, uncles and cousins from Los Angeles, grade school friends of Chris's parents, and their college-aged kids from Palo Alto all converged at the ranch. Built in the 1920s on over seventy acres in the Malibu Canyon, the ranch was the site of Memorial Day reunions for years.

The old clapboard house featured a "great room" with screened-in porches off both sides. Two upper bedrooms shared a bathroom, and the three other bedrooms and the other bathroom were off the lower part of the house. A small alcove off the living room and a kitchen and service porch completed the design. Standing out on the porch as dusk settled in, looking out over the oak trees and down towards the creek, you could hear the stream bubbling over its rocky bottom. An old California homestead at its best, it comprised just over seventy acres of pristine land. The property was hilly and dry, dotted with oak trees and manzanita brush. A strenuous hike to the top of one of the ridges would reward the group with a view of the Pacific Ocean. As the old clapboard house with a screened-in porch began to fill that night with family and friends, I realized the long drive was worth it.

Whichever unattached male drew the short straw had to sleep on the hickeyae, built into the side of the living room wall and covered in cowhide skins. This person got to bed late, after all the games had been played, and was awakened early by whomever was scheduled to start the coffee pot and make breakfast in the morning. The hickeyae person was usually spotted grabbing a nap up at the kidney-shaped pool in the late afternoon, before the younger kids arrived for games of dibble dabble.

I'm not sure who invented that game, but it seemed like an excuse to cannonball dive onto some cousin or friend in the pool who would shriek with glee. A swimmer would jump into the deep end of the pool and place a matchstick on the drain. Swimming back up to the surface, all the players got out of the pool and circled around the pool deck. As the matchstick floated to the surface, players jumped in to try and grab the prize. Arguments ensued over who found the right floating matchstick and continued long after the older siblings grew tired of the game.

The days passed quickly, filled with meals, visiting, a hike to the meadow or the waterfall, and usually a slew of family competitions. Debates over who drew whom for tennis doubles led to a tournament that kept family debates to a minimum—if you advanced a round, you had to change partners in your next match.

A late lunch was put out at about 2:00 p.m. Afternoons stretched out before us like beach towels, perfect for napping, reading, or catching a swim up in the pool. Gradually, around 5:00 p.m., everybody headed back towards the house. Jeans and flannel shirts replaced wet bathing suits that got hung outside to dry. People began to congregate in the great room with the stone fireplace, and the closet, designed as a bar, was opened. The college students whipped up ranch specialties—vodka tonics for the adults and ginger beers for the rest of us. My boyfriend was busy taking drink orders and supervising his younger brother, who was cutting up the limes.

This was when the bridge game began in earnest. New guests were warned about the competitive nature of bridge—Grammy was a serious player with a steel trap mind, who would question other's bidding strategies. She wouldn't miss a beat, even with the single earpiece of her transistor radio broadcasting Vin Scully's play-by-play of the LA Dodgers game in her left ear. Aunt Barbara and Grandma Jean, her daughters, carried on the bridge tradition with their own competitive spirits. The fourth player had to be recruited from the guests and convinced to sit in "for just a few hands" which always turned into a rubber or two. I never learned bridge. That was intentional. The game was too competitive for me and you had to earn a place at the table.

Instead, the cousins and I would set up the mah jongg game. We were spoiled playing with Grammy's set: hand-carved bone tiles dove-tailed with bamboo backs, carried back from a trip to China, in a rosewood box with brass handles. We played the Chinese way with 144 tiles, including the seasons and flowers. At the table, we built walls, rolled the dice for East Wind, and drew the tiles for our hands. We sipped ginger beers and began to build our hands as we drew tiles from the wall and discarded the tiles that didn't fit into our strategies.

Some players tried to "go pure" by collecting only one suit, but this strategy sometimes backfired as experienced players could track what was discarded and figure out the opponent's strategies. My own hand was often a shambles, with mismatched tiles that did not make a run of three sequentially numbered tiles in the same suit or a set of three matching tiles that could help score points. As the new girl learning the game, I didn't quite have the timing down yet of choosing which tiles to pick up and which to discard. Play was fast and any table talk was a distraction. The players who built their hands with tiles that matched, passed me by. Indecision left me with mismatched tiles that didn't score any points.

Instead, I announced my discard, "green dragon."

"Green dragon. It's too early in the game for that tile. Are you almost out?"

"Green dragon."

"Another one? Well, that tile's dead; here, have another one," one of the cousins commented as she discarded her green dragon.

The bridge players had started eavesdropping in earnest.

"Who's discarding all those dragons over there? Isn't it too early in the game for that?" my future mother-in-law commented.

21

As the newcomer, I cringed.

"Ah, what game are you playing, Mom? Are you at this table or over there?" My boyfriend ran some interference for me. I clenched my jaw, trying to catch his eye, and mouthed "thanks" to him.

I quickly learned this was a family of very strong and vocal women who talked over each other at the bridge table while they bid their hands. Eventually, I learned to navigate these conversations.

During these games, I appreciated Chris's willingness to step in and interrupt the conversations at the bridge table. As a guest and new to mah jongg, I was a novice. I had nothing to teach the others at my table. If I made a mistake in game strategy, I could learn from it. Chris sensed that I needed more time to understand the nuances of the game before I could begin winning hands. We were both naturally competitive and I now realize this was probably the beginning of using our own competitiveness to forge a partnership that would eventually last decades.

The game players took a break when dinner began. Most nights, it was hardy fare for large groups—lasagna, barbecued chicken, or ribs. Aunt Barbara had us sign up for planned meals before the weekend started to avoid duplication. After dinner, we kids did the clean-up, and sang many rounds of Beach Boys songs while we snapped dish towels at each other. We finished our chores, and another round of mah jongg began, or we switched to charades. This was in the days before boxed sets of topics became available, so we would tear up paper and write out titles of movies or books to act out. The actual acting-out part of charades was just a postscript for this group, the real fun was thinking up and arguing over the most obscure and difficult-to-act-out book and movie titles. "Roget's Thesaurus" and "Nancy Drew and the Case of the

Missing Glass Slipper" were always good for spirited debates about their acceptability as titles before the game started.

Once we were married, and as our own sons grew up, our Memorial Days became filled with Little League games and backyard barbecues at home. We played mah jongg on Sunday afternoons and Aunt Barbara would join us for a family dinner. Our boys learned the game, and the sound of the click of the tiles on the table reminded me of the games we played so long ago at the ranch. The ranch was eventually sold and sometimes I wondered if we had taught our sons not to discard the green dragon too soon.

That night, so many years ago, after finishing the dishes and the games about midnight, we said our goodnights and headed off to our respective bunk areas—boys in one of the back rooms, girls in the other one. As the house settled itself, quiet took over. The crickets were still chirping and, on the far side of the canyon, I heard a coyote howling. I could hear Aunt Barbara get up and check on the dogs. It was late and they needed to be inside the screened-in front porch.

The head of my bed was against the wall and I realized Chris's bunk was right on the other side. I heard him stir and whisper through the slatted wooden wall, "Babes, are you awake?"

"Sort of," I whispered.

"I think I love you."

A pause.

Careful not to wake the cousins, I replied, "I love you, too."

The dogs were scratching and settling on the front porch while Aunt Barbara puttered in the kitchen. She switched off the back porch light and my dreams took over.

View from the Endzone

I N THE FALL OF 1973, my college crush on Chris was in full bloom. He was my graduate school boyfriend and when he knocked on the door, my heart raced and my skin would get tingly. This tall, long-haired swimmer and sailor with two capped front teeth asked me to go to a football game with him. I couldn't stop smiling.

That afternoon, we walked through the southside campus neighborhood and cut up to Telegraph Avenue. Young people in tie-dye shirts and long, flowing skirts with handmade necklaces were cooking soup on Svea stoves and sharing joints. Backpacks doubled as cushions for street people perched on their haunches next to sleeping bags. The air smelled sweet. Free-spirited, bare-chested philosophers in bell bottoms floated past us. Meanwhile, up on Sproul Plaza, academic types in khakis and navy-blue blazers walked purposefully as they headed toward the libraries. The energy of this hodgepodge campus community captivated me. I wanted to be one of them.

As we held hands, Chris and I meandered across campus from tailgate to tailgate and made new friends along the way. He handed out beers from a canvas Co-op grocery bag to a group that offered us chips and salsa. Card tables, decorated in school colors with blue and gold tablecloths and silver candelabras with blue candles, sagged under the weight of six packs of beer, bottles of wine, and party platters. "Bad, Bad Leroy Brown" blared from a boom box. Spontaneous dance moves, sing-alongs, and college drinking songs popped up all around us. Dance partners were optional, everyone knew the lyrics.

Nearby, the University of California Marching Band, over 200 strong, assembled on Sproul Plaza. Dressed in their traditional wool uniforms, they looked too hot for an early September Saturday. The brass section and the drums announced the start of their march as they high stepped in formation, trickles of sweat drizzling down their cheeks. We stepped aside and let the band pass on their way up the hill to California Memorial Stadium.

Families and friends joined us as we continued our trek along the paved walkways that crisscrossed campus and led up to the stadium. The game day enthusiasm heated up as kick-off approached. Shouts of "Go Bears!" echoed through Strawberry Canyon.

We fell in step behind the band and finally reached the stadium, trudging up four flights of stairs to our seats in the north end zone. We slapped each other's backs and high fived, excited as we waited for our team to make its entrance onto the field.

The cannon fired. The boom echoed across the canyon and signaled the beginning of the pregame routine. The drum major high-stepped his way to the fifty-yard line as the marching band members ran in formation through the tunnel and followed him onto the field. Standing during the National Anthem, most of us had a hand across our chests. As the band cleared the field and moved up into their seats in the student rooting section, the cannon blasted again, and puffs of smoke rose. Our Golden Bear players and coaches ran out of the north tunnel, busting through the fog and running to the far sideline. The late arriving undergraduate students filled the stands above the home team benches. Meanwhile, the visiting team exited their locker room from under the southwest side of the stadium and jogged to their sideline. They were welcomed with a weak cheer from their outnumbered fans.

At last, the players, coaches, referees, and fans were ready. The game day captains met at midfield for the coin toss. The referee's mic shorted out and it was hard to hear his garbled instructions to the team captains. The Bears would defend the north end zone first and kick off. After handshakes, the captains rejoined their respective teams on the sidelines. Final words from each coach, and the starting players ran out to take their positions on the field. Our group was jumping up and down on the benches; we had been waiting nine months for this kick-off. We could barely hear the referee's whistle, but it didn't matter. The ball was kicked, and the first game of the season began.

Our group sat down and collectively caught our breaths. We shared Chris's binoculars. Our longitudinal view of the field meant we could see the plays on the field develop as the quarterback saw them. The quarterback looked right. The defense shifted slightly as he held his gaze; he quickly jerked his helmet left and threw a rocket of a pass towards the opposite sideline to a receiver who had gained a step on his defender. The first play from scrimmage was a success; the Bears gained eight yards. As fans, we knew this was an indication of a great victory to come. Our early season enthusiasm bubbled over; we teased each other that this would be our Rose Bowl year. By the second quarter my voice was hoarse.

I was mesmerized. Each time the ball was snapped, a choreographed play executed by eleven offensive players began. Sudden motion: a passer and receivers challenged the opponent's huge linemen and quick defensive backs. These pass routes were tricky to run and catching the ball was never a given. Even a handoff could get bobbled. Potential miscues lurked around each play. Any one of those plays could have led to a touchdown, hopefully, for our team.

My infatuation with football had an unassuming beginning. Being a "sporty" girl, I had gravitated towards the "feminine" sports at the time—tennis, volleyball, softball, field hockey, and basketball, where I played "rover." In high school, basketball for girls was played on a divided court and positions were split up so only two out of six players could be "rovers" or full-court players. The idea at that time was the half-court player's positions protected girls from overexertion.

It was easy for me to become a Cal fan. Football didn't have exertion restrictions. Watching it represented something new to me. The physicality of the college game was unlike the high school sports I had watched. This was a competition of brains and brawn that was mesmerizing. Initially, I had trouble following the plays, but with Chris by my side on those Saturday afternoons, I learned the terminology and strategies of the game. Drop back passers, quarterback draws, the tight end over the middle, and cross blocking schemes suddenly began to make perfect sense.

After almost four hours, my boyfriend, seatmates, and I were still jumping up and down, hugging each other, clapping and chanting cheers.

"Did you see that?" we yelled at each other. On our feet, we celebrated a go-ahead touchdown, with only a few minutes left in the game.

"This is it; it's going to be our year, Rose Bowl for sure," Chris yelled.

We high-fived and kidded each other. We hadn't been to the Rose Bowl in Pasadena since 1959. Yet, we would continue our annual quest for football success in the seasons to come. Finally, the cannon fired, signaling the end of the game. All sweaty and hoarse, we were relieved to start the season with a win. Exhausted, and in search of a cold beer, I reached up and clasped Chris's hand as we made our way down the stairs. We recalled our favorite plays as we headed down the hill to his frat house to celebrate.

In later years, we would stop at the Faculty Club before the game to mingle with the older Cal fans. We would order a burger and a beer, watch a rival's football game on TV, and talk about our team's chances in that day's game with the "Old Blues". These fellow fans inspired us; we felt at ease surrounded by older folks who wore their collegiate allegiance on their sweatshirts like we did.

Benchmark plays bubble up from my memory. A flea-flicker pass from a quarterback to a fullback, who lobbed a wounded duck downfield to the tight end who was completely open on the sideline. The stadium held its collective breath. The receiver paused as he caught the ball, surprised at how open he was, and almost like fielding a punt, he pivoted, ran almost the length of the field, and scored a touchdown. The stadium erupted, and I was not alone in the blush of a renewed crush on my team.

Now, without Chris by my side, I realize that an afternoon in the stadium isn't just about football. After over forty years as a Bear fan, and with a heart that bleeds blue and gold on Saturdays, it's still about staying true to our traditions, being with family, and renewing friendships on game day. These are my people.

Now, holding hands with my grandchildren on gameday, we follow our mascot, Oski, and the band up the hill towards the stadium. I secretly hope one of them will become a future Golden Bear. Maybe then we will celebrate our team playing on New Year's Day in Pasadena, and this "Old Blue" will have saved the right faded sweatshirt to wear on game day.

First date

Early years backpacking

Friends at the ranch

Fred and Chris, backpacking dads

Our young skiers

Three generations of Woodwards

III. SNAGS

The First Goodbye

THANK GOODNESS FOR FRIENDS and credit cards. A few days after Chris's death, I arrived on the East Coast. Rob and Sue, college friends, met me at the airport. They were perfect hosts and knew what to do and when. They fed me, supported me, and let me rest. What could have been a dreary trip filled with depressing end-of-life tasks instead became an experience of shared compassion as we reminisced about our friendships over the years.

We remembered the time Chris "lost" his car in the Zeta parking lot and called the police to report it stolen. Chris and Rob were groomsmen in each other's weddings, and we danced the night away at each other's receptions. When our children were small, they visited our mountain cabin and the guys skied with our firstborn kids between their legs. We recalled the times we traveled to Cal football games only to come up one touchdown short of a victory, again. These were wonderful memories, and for a moment, these conversations shielded me from the shock of losing Chris.

This was also the first time Chris's death became real in the sense that I saw how it affected his friends. Rob had hosted the board dinner the night before Chris died. He and Chris overlapped in college and, with MBA's from Berkeley, they had a lot in common. But more importantly to me, as members of the same fraternity, they were each other's brother.

Slowly, I began to understand that the well of grief I had fallen into was really an ocean that would include the grief of our family members, friends, acquaintances, colleagues, golf and hiking buddies, little league coaches and umpires. Then there were the people Chris knew whom I never met. I shuddered at the sheer number of his friendships and began to wonder how I would ever be able to hold my own grief together when so many others around me would be grieving, too.

We had a quiet dinner at their home, and I collapsed in the antique bed, with mountains of quilts on it, in the upstairs guest room. I felt bone tired, but I knew I was lucky that they provided a comfortable and supportive place for me to land. That night, I felt safe with my friends. Their compassion was the currency of friendship, and I was able to sleep for more than an hour at a time that night. I was apprehensive about what lay ahead. In the morning, we would go to the mortuary. I had talked with the mortuary owner on the phone before my flight and asked him to just lay Chris out and cover him in quilts. I did not want to see him in a casket, as he would be cremated.

The mortuary had a parking lot that overlooked a river, but as we approached the building, it looked a little tired around the edges. Inside the reception area, the wood paneling looked fake, the carpet needed a cleaning, the flowers were plastic.

The funeral director's son greeted us. He offered his condolences and led us into a conference room. I was mesmerized by the fullness of his hair, and I couldn't decide if it was a hairpiece or natural. I was so distracted staring at his hair that I could barely concentrate when he started to go through all the costs of viewing Chris, his cremation, and the shipping charges involved. He asked how I was going to pay for them. I pulled out my wallet and credit card, the one with the balance below its limit. Abruptly, he stood up, reached for my card and went upstairs. Returning quickly, he announced that my credit card cleared, as though he had magically made that happen. His awkwardness was disconcerting.

Handing me my card, he offered his condolences once again.

He then asked, "Are you ready to see your father?"

"What???" I blurted out. Did I just hear that? He had my full attention now. I started to feel panicky, like a trapped animal. What was I doing here?

In a moment of clarity, I snapped "That's my husband in there, not my father!"

Rob was aghast, looked at me, and stood up. "I'll take care of this," he said.

I needed to see my husband now. I pushed my chair back as I stood up.

I entered the room where he was laid to rest and impulsively started running over to him. He seemed asleep but wasn't snoring. His skin was still pinkish and a little shiny. This was the beginning of his death mask and I was relieved to see he didn't appear traumatized. Rather, he seemed peaceful, somehow taller, longer than usual. Maybe it was the way they layered the quilts on him.

I hugged his chest and gasped for air. I knelt on a riser and started to pray. I was sort of crying, trying to pray, but I still had things I needed to say to him. "How could you do this? This wasn't supposed to happen now. We're supposed to go to Idaho in two weeks for a vacation, did you forget that? What about the boys? What about me?"

I felt like someone else was talking. I tried to breathe. I needed to get a grip on my emotions. Gradually, I just stood next to him and looked down, just wishing things could be different.

Our friends had been waiting patiently and wanted to go in and say their goodbyes as well. I silently nodded as I passed them on my way out. I went to sit outside so they could have some private time. When they came out, I went back inside to say one last goodbye.

I have never been good at goodbyes. Sentimentality sneaks up on me, and over the years, I have usually cried at goodbyes, and at some wonderful hellos. But this was different. I could see Chris was dead and was not going to be walking in the front door, calling out his big "hello" ever again. My mistake was thinking this would be my last goodbye to him. Instead, it would be the first of many goodbyes, through the ensuing years. All I could see was a lot of emptiness in my future.

Standing close to him in the viewing room, I leaned over and hugged him for the last time. Finally, I felt cried out. I said my final prayer and last goodbye, thanking him for the life we shared and the gift of our three sons. I walked out of the mortuary dry-eyed.

My friends were sitting in Adirondack chairs looking out over the Farmington River. We decided to just sit for a few minutes; I slowly started to think in different terms. I was not part of a team any longer. The matriarch of our family now, I began to realize the weight of the responsibilities I would face in the future. I didn't know exactly what I would have to face as a new widow, but I did know I was strong and resilient. All those years of junior and collegiate college competitions, when I had to maintain steely resolve during tennis matches, prepared me well. I would need those traits to face what lay ahead.

Silently, we walked to their car and went to the local police station. I needed to claim Chris's personal effects—his wallet, phone, car keys, watch, and his wedding ring. A plastic evidence bag contained the jogging shoes and workout clothes he had on that morning. We headed back to the house. Chris's personal things from the motel room, his carry-on bag, along with some clothes that were left on the floor in the motel room that morning, were spread out on the floor in Rob's home office. I realized that I would be carrying my deceased husband's personal effects home.

The next morning, over coffee, we decided how to spend my last day there. Rob wanted to know if I wanted to see the reservoir where Wood probably ran that last morning and where, on the road back to the motel, he died. I gulped and said yes. He knew I would need this closure. I changed into my exercise clothes, we got in the car and headed towards the reservoir. Rob knew Chris's routines; this was where he usually ran, as it was close to the motel.

Parking in the lot, we got out of the car. Rob and Sue decided to walk around the lake in a clockwise direction, I decided to jog in the opposite direction. I sensed I needed to do this by myself. I needed to be where he was, to experience what the morning light would have been like through the trees, to see the water, placid, as there was no wind. We took off in opposite directions.

The parking lot had only a few cars in it; it was still early. Just a few people were out walking. The trail was a fire road, wide enough for a truck, of well-worn dirt and rocks. The trees and grasses that surrounded the reservoir provided some shade for the walkers. A very slight breeze came up and caused the water to ripple. Anxiously I started out too fast, but gradually slowed down and settled into a moderate jogging pace.

About half-way around, we crossed paths. I marveled at their closeness, holding hands as they walked. I was comforted that they would have a future to share together. I continued around, and as I neared the end of the loop, a pair of turkeys crossed my path. They were big, brown, and walked close together. They paused as I jogged towards them. We had a moment where we stopped and stared at each other. I was a little startled at their large size and they both turned, a matched pair, dismissive, and continued across the path. I took their presence as a message that Chris was sending me— while I am not with you at this moment, I am never far away.

My friends and I met up again at the parking lot, and on the car ride home, we drove by the spot where the police found Chris in his rental car. A thoroughfare, with cars zipping by. He had pulled off the road and the car had come to a stop on a grass easement alongside a six-foot fence in front of a home. The pullout is indistinguishable from others along the roadway. Another level of reality set in.

The commonness of this setting was so out of character for someone who was so passionate about the outdoors; I always envisioned his death would occur after a day of hiking or skiing, standing on top of some mountain, savoring the view. But that day I realize he had not died as a mountain man, out skiing, hiking, or exploring. Instead, of all places, he died along the side of a road, in a rental car. I struggled to understand the ordinary way he died with the exceptional way he lived.

The next morning, Rob dropped me off at the airport. I headed home, appreciating friendships, and I started to realize what an incredible life I had with Chris. The friends, the travels, the football games, the adventures with the kids—his life was a life well lived. As was mine, with him by my side.

On the flight home, I slowly realized Chris no longer belonged to only me.

Day-to-Day

O N MAY DAY, THE fog started to lift and revealed the city across the bay with just a hint of morning chill in the air. Nine months had slipped by since Chris passed away. The breeze evoked memories of sailing with Chris across the whitecaps in Southern California before we started our family. Eventually, our weekends were spent unloading the boys' tricycles at Aquatic Park and walking along the Berkeley Marina with them, throwing dried scraps of sourdough bread to the gulls. Those early family days before the boys began organized sports programs, especially baseball, were long ago.

This morning, our oldest son, Alex, and I headed up to the Caldecott Sports Field to see the bench with Chris's name etched into its back. Walking up the easement that ran along the road gave us some time to remember Chris. Each of us was still in the initial stages of grief. Sometimes we discussed a special moment we shared with Chris, other times we walked quietly alongside each other, without a need to talk. He was grieving deeply and, as a parent, I wished there were some way I could ease the pain of losing his dad so suddenly and too soon. At the nine-month mark, we still could not believe Chris was gone. It seemed like just a few days ago we were expecting him home from his business trip. Alex recounted that they were supposed to get together on that Saturday for lunch, the day he and Elana returned home from their babymoon holiday. Instead of preparing for that lunch, he learned of his father's death.

The benches acknowledged eight coaches and volunteers who each contributed 25 or more years of service to North Oakland Little League. The league's board had made such a nice gesture, recognizing Chris for his volunteer service. But I felt anxious in anticipation of seeing his bench for the first time. I was saddened, knowing he would never see this tribute.

We reminisced not only about the time we did have with Chris, but also about how much time his volunteer activities kept him away from the family. As the boys outgrew many of the junior leagues and teams he helped by coaching, mentoring, scheduling, and serving on the board, he continued his service to the league. We recognized Chris's love of sports, especially baseball. He left behind a legacy of teaching young people, not only the skills of the game, but also the sportsmanship and respect for their opponents that went along with sports.

At the bench, we sat down and caught our breaths. We both got teary. I rubbed my hand along the cutout letters of his name and wished I could hear his voice and feel his hug just one more time. The bench was placed in a beautiful spot, along the third baseline behind a chain link fence, so no overthrows at third base would hit the spectators here. The playing field had recently been dragged and striped, ready for the next game. We scanned the hills; we basked in the view all the way out to San Francisco Bay and the Golden Gate Bridge. Alex and I reminisced about our family's shared love of baseball, and all the games when he had worked the bases for Chris. We remembered Chris's routine of putting the chest protector and shin guards on and stepping around the backstop. He would have paused and looked to his right and seen the same view we were sharing that morning. Before he turned his baseball hat backwards and slipped the umpire's mask straps over the back of his head, he'd pull down on the chin strap to adjust it and then tighten the straps from the side. After suiting up, he was ready to start the game.

Chris had probably spent years in volunteer time in that dugout, coaching, pacing along the third baseline, sending signals to the first base runner, and eventually umpiring behind the plate. He knew this view, and now we could sit on his bench and feel close to him and the game of baseball he loved so much. When I sit on his bench, I can almost hear his voice as he turned to the visiting team with the call: "Batter up!" Once the player dug in at the plate and was ready, Chris would have pointed at the pitcher and yelled, "Play ball."

As I looked across the diamond at the benches, and farther out to the Bay, I knew the bench was a tribute to him for his service, but over time I suspected it would become a memorial bench for our family. Now it is a place where we can meet, appreciate the view, reflect on Chris's love of baseball, and sometimes even see a game in progress. I sense he would have liked that.

Sitting there, Alex and I couldn't help remembering one of Chris's favorite baseball quotes. Growing up in Southern California, he listened to the Dodgers games with his grandmother and her black transistor radio. He loved Vin Scully's broadcasts of the games. Listening to his broadcasts in our own home, he would often clap his hands hard to punctuate a good play or a home run. His favorite quote was from the 1991 season, when the Dodgers played the Chicago Cubs, and Vin Scully announced the next batter: "Andre Dawson has a bruised knee and is listed as day-to-day. (pause) Aren't we all?" *

Savoring that memory and Chris's love of the game, we slowly stood up and began the walk back down the hill.

* Source: On-air radio broadcast (1991)

Scanning the Ridgeline

C LEANING OUT CHRIS'S BOX of maps was a gut check. The plastic box, missing its top, was stuffed to its brim with USGS topographic maps collected over forty years. They were folded to the last quadrant of our trips because he never bothered to refold them when he tossed them into the box once we returned home. His map box left a real-time history of completed adventures as well as new maps for hikes that were still to come. Sometimes, the planned route on the map was highlighted, but I knew better.

The last time I was able to backpack with Chris, James joined us in the Ansel Adams Wilderness. The first day was tame for us. Parking near the trailhead from one of the west entrances to the wilderness area, we followed the trail down a long, steep grade until we finally arrived at a small lake where we pitched our tents. My creaky hip was sore, and the weight of my pack and the pitch of the downslope had put a lot of pressure on my joint over our five-hour afternoon. But the lake where we stopped was beautiful and ringed with trees. A cooling breeze gently sculpted the water as we set up our tents, purified some water and settled in to read in the late afternoon light. I even had time to soak my hip in the lake, the cool water soothing some of the ache in the joint.

The next morning, we were up early, looking forward to a full day's hike. Chris had planned the route following a trail. We followed it until lunchtime. But, by midday, he was tired of looping around a boulder field and started to try to convince us that, if we just cut through the boulder field, we could save time to get to our next campsite. By then, my hip was really aching. Even changing my gait so slightly and shortening my stride did not relieve the pain. Clearly, I had not brought enough Ibuprofen. The increasing size of the boulders was intimidating. I could not envision being able to boulder hop across this field. The trail seemed like a good route for me.

In the wilderness, the three of us reached an impasse. Chris really wanted to cut across the boulder field. I could see the ridgeline he wanted to get to, but I was uncertain about the way there and whether my hip could withstand the uneven footing necessary to cut across the rocks. For the first time in my hiking life with Chris, I mutinied. I refused to budge and made it clear I was not going to follow him across the boulder field. James was unusually quiet. I said I was heading back to last night's campsite and would stay there until they returned in two to three days.

Our son made his own decision; I had company as we retraced our steps and headed back to camp. Late in the afternoon, we crossed paths with a group of young women who were out for their first backpacking experience. Their enthusiasm was contagious. They were laughing as their pots, pans, bags of cutlery and numerous water bottles clipped to the outside of their packs clanged together as they hiked. Their two guides, trekkers with much smaller packs and a lot of hiking miles etched into their weathered cheeks, caught up with us. We exchanged greetings, the new hikers all tried to talk simultaneously. James and I marveled at their eagerness. Eventually we shared with their group what trailhead we had started at and where we were headed for that night.

This chance encounter on the trail buoyed our spirits as James and I turned and continued our way back to our campsite. It was fun to chat with these outdoor enthusiasts on their first trip to the backcountry, an experience we hoped they would continue to enjoy in seasons to come.

James and I also talked about when I first started hiking with Chris, reminiscing about my first pack, a red Universal, exterior-framed pack that was probably just as stuffed as the gals' packs were. When I was new to backpacking, I always carried too much gear. But over the years, I learned to take just the essentials. Yet, I was still learning. I had not anticipated the hike's impact on my arthritic hip, and I was hurting. Plus, we had split from our guide, a decision not recommended in the backcountry. We arrived back at our campsite in the late afternoon and dropped our packs to the ground. I kept mulling over my decision to split up, and hoped I would not regret it.

Later that evening, as James and I were setting up the stove to boil water for packaged soup, Chris walked into camp. He had cut across the boulder field, ditching his green Kelty pack as he scrambled up the last hundred feet to the ridgeline to take in the view. Relieved at his arrival, I imagined his profile on the ridge, his hiking hat with the sweat stains along the brim, shading his eyes as he scanned the distant ridges and meadows below. I was relieved and glad he was back in camp, but I also realized these trips were becoming too strenuous for me as my hip still hurt.

We spent the next day relaxing. We took dips in the lake, read and napped. The fourth day, we climbed the long uphill trail back to the parking lot and drove home. Sitting in the front seats of our old blue VW Vanagon, we discussed that I couldn't do these trips anymore. He would be on his own to do them with our sons and various hiking friends. We were both relieved that a truce had been reached.

The dad-and-son hiking adventures picked up the following summer. Chris dutifully marked a trailhead as a meeting place for others to join him. These hikes included our sons, Chris's best friend—also a father—his sons, and sometimes a friend or two of the boys. I wouldn't join these trips as they were too strenuous for me even when my hip wasn't so arthritic. Besides, dads and sons needed guy time together.

I encouraged these adventures. My role was to drop the hikers off at the trailhead and show up seven days later, to pick them up. Often another mom would join me in a separate car, transporting the hikers and their gear to the trailhead. Dropping the group off was easy, the guys were clean and eager to begin the hike. Our goodbyes were brief.

Returning home in a silent VW bus to an empty house meant a week of hoping all was going well on the trail.

Meeting the group a week later was always a relief, and fun. Despite how dusty and sweaty they were, my hugs for the adventurers lasted a few seconds too long—and were sometimes embarrassing. We would head to a brew pub with outdoor seating in some mountain town, so the guys could relax and refuel with a burger and a beer. Slowly, the stories would come out, usually censored, so as not to worry the other mom and me about their safety. Tales of sprained ankles and falls with heavy packs would come out in the weeks to come.

While sorting through the maps, I didn't assume Chris followed the yellow highlighted routes. I knew that at some point, he would divert and bushwhack, having convinced the others that if they just clambered through this canyon and scaled that hillside, everyone could cut through that opening on the crest of the ridge and scramble down the other side. I could imagine his words. He would have been convincing the group, rationalizing how much mileage and time they could save. Shortcuts always sounded like a good idea at the beginning, and being hot, sweaty, and thirsty, who wouldn't want to save some time and mileage? Besides, it always meant more time in the afternoon for reading in camp or twilight fishing at a lake.

But bushwhacking was not easy, and it didn't always feel like a shortcut. Instead of following a well-worn trail, etched into the mountain by native people generations ago, by animals, by mule and horse trains, possibly by park rangers and hundreds of other hikers, Chris had to forge his own way. He often had the others convinced of the value of cutting through a new route. Yet, every single step of bushwhacking was a decision: left, right, up, down. This was tiring enough by itself as foot plants must be steady and deliberate to hold and maintain one's balance. Bushwhacking may have saved mileage, but it rarely saved time or energy.

The hikes were strenuous, and bushwhacking became what Chris was known for in the backcountry. But reaching the crest of a mountain and seeing a view perhaps no one before him had ever seen was an inspiring reward. The boys would report back to me, "Yeah, Mom, we only bushwhacked one day out of six on the trail. It was hard; so-and-so sprained his ankle. Drew took a very scary fall but was okay; we all made it to the top. Yes, the view was worth it, but it really is a Dad thing."

With the heart of an explorer, it was hard for Chris to follow a well-marked trail.

Knowing how he loved to explore, it was even more shocking for me to learn that he died after a morning run around a reservoir. There was a well-worn path and possibly other runners out that morning with him. In the rental car, as he pulled over to the side of the road, his life slipped away. I could only hope that his last vision was a view from a mountaintop. As a true scout, he would have been scanning the ridgelines and the meadows, rivers, lakes, and trees below. That expansive view from the top of a mountain would have been his alone, and it would have brought him a sense of wonder and accomplishment.

I Should Have Known

FTER A YEAR INTO my grief, I was almost able to talk about Chris and his love of the boys and outdoor adventures without crying. But sadness still crept in, like that gnarly root on the trail that might cause me to stumble. A sudden flash of anger arose when he was not there to help carry in the groceries, load the dishwasher or take out the trash. Together, we ran the household, from mundane chores to hosting wonderful celebrations with friends. Alone, I was overwhelmed by household and business tasks. In a moment of frustration, I resented that he had left me alone to take care of all the seemingly endless work of settling his affairs. Yet, I knew full well he did not intend to die that day.

A year and a half before he died, the two of us were skiing at Palisades Tahoe, at that time called Squaw Valley. I usually didn't like to ski there, especially as I got older. The mountain was big and in places very steep. Even as I skied on the edge of intermediate runs, away from the congestion of skiers clogging the middle of the trails, I found the young, hotshot skiers intimidating. I would hear them come up behind me, only to pass just a little too close on either side as I headed down the slope. But we had corporate coupons that day, so we headed to Palisades Tahoe.

Taking a noontime break, we headed to Gold Coast for lunch. The lodge was packed, but, luckily, we got seats inside facing each other, as the outside deck was full. Chris went to buy a beer and a soda and I pulled out our sandwiches and apples from our skiing daypack.

Coming back, he sat down and took a gulp of beer as I unwrapped our sandwiches. I was chatting away and looked across the table at him. He was staring at me, but there was no recognition in his eyes; they seemed glazed over. I called to him, "Chris, Chris," in a louder voice, and he slid off his stool and fell to the floor. Like on a movie set, I stood up and started yelling, "Is there a doctor in the house?" I crossed over to his side of the table. He was lying on his side on the floor and there was no way I could lift him.

Men started to surround me, saying, "Here, let me help; the ski patrol is on its way." I looked up and two young men in red jackets arrived. Chris started to regain consciousness, but he seemed woozy and he wasn't sure what had happened. The ski patrollers propped him upright on the floor and tried to get him up on the stool. This whole incident took maybe two minutes. The patrollers were reassuring, trying to calm us and explaining that this wasn't that unusual an occurrence. The other skiers moved away from us and got back to their lunches. I looked at Chris again. His eyes were starting to focus more and his gasping breath had become more regular. Finally, he was sitting up on his own.

The ski patrollers outlined a plan. They talked to each of us separately. One would take Chris down in the gondola to the first aid station; the other patroller would help me get our skis and poles from the racks outside the lodge and we'd go down in the second gondola. I was wearing our backpack. We left our lunch and drinks on the table, and the patroller headed out to get our gear and guided me towards the second gondola.

We had never downloaded in the gondola before. A badge of courage for us was to ski down the mountain at the end of the day, regardless of the weather or snow conditions. Somehow, this ride felt surreal; the motion of going down was like floating through the air. We got down to the base of the mountain and off-loaded. The ski patrollers walked us to the first aid station. We left our gear outside, and they made sure Chris got checked into the clinic. I turned to say thank you, but they had already turned away and were walking towards the funitel. I watched them cut discreetly into the line and duck into a cabin to ride back up the hill.

Chris was taken into a private room. I trailed behind and stood in the doorway. His color was looking better already. He was sitting up on the table and answering questions. The doctor began listening to his heart and lungs. He thought Chris had had an episode of vasovagal syncope, possibly a reaction to the cold beer he had gulped, dropping his blood pressure, and causing the fainting spell. The doctor was not concerned. He told us people passing out on the ski slope was not that uncommon, but because this was the first time it had happened to Chris, he insisted Chris consult with his own doctor. He spoke only to Chris, but I heard the instructions, too. The doctor signed off on his observations and handed the evaluation to Chris.

We left the clinic together. With my skis and poles on my shoulder, I walked towards the parking lot. I didn't hear him behind me, so I turned and realized he was heading in the other direction. He looked back when he realized I was not right behind him.

"Where are you going?" I yelled.

"I'm going to ski a couple more runs on Red Dog, it's only 2:30 p.m. and the lifts will be open for another two hours."

I stared in disbelief. "What? You think this is a good time to go ski? You were just in the medical hut. I think we should go back to the cabin to rest for a while."

"No, I'm feeling fine now. Let's get a few more runs in."

I couldn't believe he was doing this, but I could believe it. He was not one to accept defeat. I couldn't believe I was doing this, either. I took one run with him on Red Dog and went down to the locker room deck, sat down and waited. My annoyance at him simmered. When he finally joined me on the deck, we headed to the car. He insisted that I promise to not tell anyone what had happened. I was incredulous and could only stare at him. I was silent in the car on our drive back to the cabin, a condition I maintained into the next day.

After Chris' death, my father saw me struggle with all the tasks that defaulted to me. Pops had been a widower for four years by then and he became a role model for me in a new way. We shared the experience of the loss of a spouse, and he became my new support system, in a way that felt different than his being my parent. We grew closer emotionally. We could talk about missing our respective spouses, the best and the worst of times with each of them, the business side of their deaths, and what lay ahead for each of us that we would have to face alone. Pops helped me understand how I could support my sons and daughters-in-law in their grief, as he had supported my brothers and me after the death of our mom.

Pops had his own grieving to do as well. The energetic presence Chris always was in our lives was gone for him, too. The phone calls from his son-in-law that started out with "How are you, you old fart?" were never to happen again. No more Sunday afternoons watching golf together on our many visits to Southern California, no more backyard Newport Rib Company barbecues that Chris was quick to organize, no more debating the class of a sailboat passing by our porch on a beach vacation. Pops experienced the void Chris left behind, and it made him turn inward; he became quieter and more reflective. A stoic Swede, he spent more time alone reading.

The dad who showed up with me at meetings with his legal pad and pencil after Chris died was determined that the hurdles I faced settling Chris's estate would not happen when the time came for me to settle my Dad's estate. Pops' last gift to me was to prepare me for his passing. As hard as it was for some of those conversations to occur, it was a comfort for me to know his final wishes.

So, after Chris died, almost every visit to Southern California necessitated a visit with Dad to his bank. I would sit with him in a tiny, windowless room, and together we would go through his safe deposit box, bringing tears and laughter to us both. A well-lived life, documented with birth certificates, confirmation certificates, a prayer book, a marriage license, U.S. Army discharge papers, a 10th Mountain Infantry patch and a Bronze Star, college diplomas, and my mom's death certificate, prompted his memories as he shared stories with me. During one of those visits, he made a gift to me of his and Mom's wedding bands, tied together with a little piece of white satin ribbon.

We also made visits to his attorney's office and calls to his accountant. Introductions went all around and he insisted I sit with him at his desk to review his income, expenses, details of his health directive, what his plans were for his body after he died, and where he wanted his ashes to be spread. Sitting with him at his desk and seeing how he organized his accounts made me realize this was going to be much easier than the tasks I had faced at my own home. He even maintained a monthly ledger of income, expenses, and gifts made to family members, which my mom had started in the early years of their marriage.

"I got this, Dad," I assured him.

But the silence of aloneness was deafening when I returned home from those visits. While chores and emails and paying bills filled up the time, it was the silence of being the only one home that was loudest. The refrigerator hummed along and the ice cubes dropped into the storage bin, marking time. Gone were the shared moments of a hug at the door, the stories of a surprise accomplishment at work, or the easy banter about the starting pitcher for the local baseball team. My life, the one I had lived in tandem with Chris for forty years, inched along in silence.

I should have known what to expect after Chris's episode at Palisades Tahoe. He could not face his own fragility, much less his own mortality. It was of no comfort for me that he died without us having a final plan in place for what I was to do after his death. I should have known better. He avoided conversations about what I should do if he died first, and instead labeled me a worrier.

That episode in the first aid hut began a year of reminding, begging, cajoling him to go see the doctor. He finally acquiesced. I suspected he and the doctor had a nice conversation comparing recent backpacking trips instead of any hidden health problems. That is usually what Chris reported they talked about. When he came back home after this visit, he shared the advice from his doctor to keep exercising and eating well. He was a picture of health, with no medications needed. He had the good sense not to add "I told you so. ..."

I continued to rewind different scenarios of our life and wondered if I could have done something, anything, to prevent his sudden death a year and a half after that episode at the ski lodge. What could I have fixed that would have changed the outcome for him that morning? As I continued to look back, I realized even if I had been there on a run with him that morning, I could not have saved him. He was too big for me to lift out of the car, my chest compressions wouldn't have been strong enough to restart his heart, help could not have reached us in time. He didn't even have his cell phone with him that morning.

Eventually, I would learn to live with the silence he left

behind. The coroner assured me he died within two minutes, barely knowing what was happening. But I could only imagine. I would never know if his life flashed before him, or if his chest hurt, or if he was afraid. After over forty years of intertwined lives, I only knew I was not there for his last run. And, just like when he picked me up in his Fairlane on that first date so many years ago, the police report noted when they found him in the rental car, the engine was still running.

The Last Three Miles

LOOKING BACK, IN THOSE first few months after Chris's death, I experienced periods of constant shaking. I felt my metabolism speeding along, rest didn't calm it. The shock of losing him was visceral; I lost eight pounds in a few weeks and could sleep only two hours at a time. I finally realized I needed to take care of myself and went to see my doctor. She prescribed antidepressants, but I declined. Instead, I asked for referrals to grief counselors. Maybe, if I talked with someone, it would help relieve my anxiety so my body and heart could begin to heal.

I left a few voicemails for the first referral. I explained my situation and left both my home and work phone numbers for her to call me. She never responded. I tried again and left a message for the second referral. That therapist did respond, and in a phone conversation we had one evening, she decided I didn't match the demographic of her grief groups. She worked with mostly eighty-year-olds grieving the loss of a spouse from a terminal illness. She was unable to refer me to anyone else.

My grief was compounded by my isolation. I couldn't think of anyone with a similar experience to talk with about the grief I was experiencing. Finally, I took a deep breath, closed the door to my office and called the campus health center. I scheduled an appointment with a therapist for the following week and felt a little more hopeful.

Walking across campus to the appointment, I was careful not to run into any of my colleagues. We were part of a work group, pushed hard by metrics and goals for the amounts of money we raised for campus programs and scholarships. I was motivated to contribute to the team's success, so I didn't want anyone to see me in a vulnerable moment, seeking help. I felt relieved and a little bit brave as I walked across campus to the meeting. I was hopeful this would be the connection I needed to explore my grieving process.

After a few pleasantries and introductory questions, the therapist looked at me and said, "You don't look like you need counseling. You'll be fine."

I was shocked at her assessment. After only ten minutes of talking to me, she decided I didn't need grief counseling. What did she think I was in her office for? It felt like I had been punched in the heart. Sure, I was in my business clothes, black slacks, a collared blue shirt, and blue blazer. But still, I was asking for help. I walked out of her office deflated.

Instead of returning to the office, I walked back to my car. I got in and sat in the driver's seat. I started to cry. The tears wouldn't stop. It seemed even when I asked for help, I was turned away. My crying eventually eased. I used the gym towel on the floor of the car to wipe my tears away. It was still early afternoon, so I started to think about returning to the office. Instead, I just sat in the car, realizing once again that I was on my own.

I gave up asking for help. I turned inward. Closing ranks, I decided to refocus and to love and support our sons and daughters-in-law, who were also grieving. I returned to exercising more regularly and ate a healthier diet. I developed stronger bonds within a smaller friendship group. I put other friendships that were in a more distant circle on hold. I needed to heal myself.

Years later, a therapist friend was sad to hear this story. She guessed that the university therapist thought I presented as an "apparent competence" case, that I showed signs of being in control. I certainly didn't feel in control and could only think that if the counselor had asked a few more questions, she would have understood my reluctance to appear vulnerable at work. I was asking for help, and I yearned to understand grief better. I also wanted to connect with others experiencing loss.

Later that week, after my failure to find a therapist who would work with me, the dream started. Up until that point, I had not been sleeping long enough to have dreams. In the middle of the night, I was startled awake by the three warning bells on our front door opening: ding, ding, ding. I sat up in bed and thought Chris was walking in through the front door, returning home from his business trip. He was in his jeans, white shirt, blue blazer, and loafers. He set his carry-on down on the tile floor in the entry. Then, in a haze, I remembered . . . no, no . . . he isn't ever coming home again. But I couldn't help myself; I couldn't distinguish the dream from reality.

I slipped out of bed and went downstairs to check the front door. It was still locked. Heading back upstairs, I crawled into my side of the bed, where I still slept. I rationalized still sleeping on "my side" by thinking the reading light was better on that side of the bed. But deep down in my heart, I knew I was keeping a place for him in our bed, just in case he returned.

The dream repeated itself multiple times over the next year and caused me a deep sadness. I was upset, but also somehow comforted that Chris was trying to return home to me. As much as he traveled, he hadn't forgotten me. In my brain fog, I knew he was dead and would not be coming back home, but my heart refused to sync up with my brain. It would be another year before I could scooch over towards the middle of the bed to sleep.

A few years after Chris's death, an email startled me. My health care provider was forming a grief hiking group. I read the email and hesitated. So why am I getting this message now? The notice looked interesting enough, but shouldn't I be over my grief by now? Why wasn't this resource available when I needed it two years ago? However, recently retired, I could meet midweek at a local park and hike. I thought maybe I should try it. I decided to reply and got the details for the meetup.

I drove through the Berkeley hills and finally found the meeting spot. I parked, grabbed my poles and day pack out of the back of the car, and walked up to the picnic table. Some people were greeting other hikers, while some, like me, were waiting for the introductions to begin.

The host, Chela, a bereavement counselor, and her assistant were warm and welcoming. We introduced ourselves and shared whom we were grieving. The breadth of the group's experience stunned me—my own grief had left me self-absorbed. The hikers were grieving a wide range of losses. Some were grieving a parent, a child, a companion, a friend, a spouse, or a miscarriage. The participants ranged from those who were new to grief to others who were a few years along their grief journey. Yet, we all fit into the group. There were those who had weathered long and painful deaths of loved ones; some, like me, had experienced sudden and unexpected loss. For the first time, I started to understand that I was not alone. While the causes of the others' grief might differ from mine, we would come to know that our experiences had more in common than not.

Our host read a poem about loss, then we headed out to hike for an hour or so. It was here, in this group, that I began to learn that I could share my grief story and hear others' stories and have compassion for their losses. Maybe it was because we were hiking along an easy trail, all walking in the same direction, that we could share our experiences candidly and honestly with each other. In some ways, regardless of the type of loss we had experienced, each of us learned we were not alone.

As the group members hiked along, we changed hiking partners and floated between individual's stories easily. I shared one of my poles with someone who was having a balance problem. At the end of the hike, we met up at the table again, shared a brief thought, and then returned to our individual lives and schedules. No one exchanged contact information; instead, the group hike appeared to be just enough support and sharing for each of us.

While the grief was intense during those first years after his death, each year that passed lessened the intensity of loss, but it didn't eliminate its presence. Our sons were grieving, too; they were developing their own traditions to keep their dad close in their lives. Each of them held memories of special moments and occasions to remember and celebrate their unique experiences with their dad. One watched a golf tournament with friends each spring, one watched a favorite movie, another one took a special run at a ski resort. Each of them continued to remember him, to celebrate a special hike each year and to commemorate the lives they shared growing up with Chris as their dad. Each of them in their own grief processes taught me that memories could be motivators.

Recently, our youngest son ran the Yosemite Half Marathon, and finished in a personal best. His wife and I walked around the event barricades and through a hilly neighborhood to arrive at the last mile marker on the course. Drew passed us almost to the minute he predicted. He looked strong and even smiled when he saw us. After the race, we met up with him and walked around the finish line park, filled with runners and family members. Only then did he speak openly of his race strategy. His wife asked him how he stayed so strong, and his answer stunned me.

"The last three miles I just channeled Dad."

I suddenly realized maybe that's what we all did. In our grief, we arrived at a place where the memory of our lost loved one motivated us to pursue activities that push our own lives forward. Without realizing what I had been doing, I had been motivated by the last selfie of Chris and me at a trailhead. It was taken in Point Reyes National Seashore four months before he died. We were both leaning into the frame, his outstretched arm held his phone. I leaned into the top of his chest, shoulder height. We both wore baseball hats that day and were smiling at the phone.

When I saw that photo recently, still taped above my desk, I recognized how it had inspired me to continue to do many of the day hikes we used to do together. Those familiar hikes still brought me joy even though Chris was not by my side. Maybe that was part of my grief journey; my recognition of the person I was within our marriage and the individual I had to become after going through such a painful loss. The familiarity of that previous life, with him by my side, now propels me to continue to live my own best life.

One early morning, with the sun not quite over the treetops yet, I bent over to retie my day hikers. I knew a morning spent outdoors on a favorite trail would bring me closer to accepting my single life. Somewhere along the way, I would pause to look up at a ridgeline, or up at a peak, or across a valley to a meadow, or up to the sky to see a hawk. It was in that moment that I would remember our life together, acknowledge my loss and still feel Chris's presence close to me. I, too, would channel his spirit, turn back to the trail, and hike on.

IV. RETURN TO THE MOUNTAINS

The Christmas Stocking

MY FIRST CHRISTMAS HOLIDAY without Chris was heartbreaking. Swagging the garland over the French doors to the deck was a two-person job. I didn't trust myself to be steady on the ladder, up so high and so alone. Any decorating that involved a ladder was postponed indefinitely. Instead, I strung the clear Christmas tree lights around the deck railings, arranged some greenery and lights on the mantle and placed some treasured Santa figurines on the side tables. Decorations were limited to eye level. My holiday theme became Christmas Lite.

I wasn't sure if I was up to the task of planning that first holiday by myself. The concern expressed in a friend's voice and her wrinkled eyebrows said it all: "Are you doing okay?"

"Well, sometimes yes, sometimes no, thanks for asking," I replied.

When I reached the task of hanging the stockings from the reindeer stands on the mantle, I hesitated. I opened the box and there it was. Chris's stocking was the top one on the pile, the final one put away last year. Seeing it made my throat constrict. I sat down on the couch, temporarily immobilized by grief. I realized this task presented a decision too delicate for me to make at that moment. Our stockings had always been hung as a pair, and the boys' stockings were hung individually until they married or had a partner.

For years, our home had been decorated with just enough holiday touches. We loved to cook and entertain. Hot mulled wine scented the kitchen. Garlands and white lights eventually replaced the tree when the kids left for college. The three-foot-tall toy soldiers, constructed and painted by my Mom and Dad, flanked the front door and the fireplace. A collection of smaller toy soldiers held court, they peeked out from bookshelves, and the Santa and reindeer pillows nestled on the couches. A stack of Christmas books sat on the coffee table and included some from Chris's and my childhoods, ready to be picked up and shared at any moment. Candles of all sizes and colors created a pine-scented glow when we entertained friends and family for drinks and holiday dinners.

I dreaded the task of decorating for my first Christmas holiday in our family home without Chris. Part of my joy was sharing it with him. He loved our celebrations, the mah jongg games, and the holiday music. He even took over the purchasing and hanging of the garlands in the living room the Sunday after Thanksgiving. He pitched in and made it so much fun to plan together. We attended holiday concerts on campus and at church. We would watch football games with the sound on mute while we listened to our CD collection of holiday performances.

Slowly, I got up from the couch and finally managed to hang the boys' and a daughter-in-law's stockings from the mantle. The special girlfriend stockings went up as well. It was their holiday too. I sat down again on the couch with Chris's and my stockings in my lap. The tears wouldn't stop. In the depths of sadness, I just couldn't do this; it had been only five months since he died. I could not hang my stocking without his. I put them both back in the box, secured the top, and put the box back in the storage closet where it remained for the rest of that Christmas season.

Coyote on the Bridge

URING THE WINTER AFTER that first Christmas, we all made an effort to spend time at our cabin and reestablish our family traditions. It felt good to share a familiar household in the mountains, surrounded by the natural beauty of pine trees, snowy peaks, icy streams, and partially frozen lakes.

Despite inviting others to join me, I didn't get any takers for snowshoeing. So, in the early afternoon I decided to head out to the trail. The morning snow flurry was over, and the snow sparkled like glitter reflecting the shining sun. It was a bluebird day, the kind that skiers love. The kids were a little concerned when I headed out by myself, but the trail was familiar. Besides, it wasn't that far from our cabin. I promised to text them when I turned around, so they would know when to expect me back.

I found my snowshoes upstairs in the closet, shoved way in the back, and the straps were tangled up with Chris's pair. They were piled up right where we left them two springs ago. I took a long breath to calm my emotions. I needed to do this walk to show myself that I could continue to enjoy outdoor activities, even if I did them alone. I headed downstairs to the garage and grabbed my ski poles.

I walked out to the road, my snowshoes hanging from the poles braced on my right shoulder. I wound around until the neighborhood road met the highway. I paused, and when there was an opening, I walked across the highway and picked up Alder Creek Road on the other side. I slogged along for another fifty yards or so as my Sorels crunched the snow, and continued past the beaver dam where we used to bring the boys when they were little.

Finally, I saw the place where I had always cut down to run or walk this trail. I crowded up next to the snow berm and started to put on my snowshoes. Trying to balance on the uneven, snowy surface, I bent over and tried to wedge my boot into the stiff plastic bindings with the nylon pulls. I stood up, took a breath, and tried again. Maybe I should have pulled the snowshoes out of the closet and into the living room to warm them up a bit before I set out. Oh well. I tucked that thought away for the next time. I was finally strapped in. I used my poles and slip-slided down the traverse to where the trail leveled out along the creek.

I paused. I had made it this far. I listened and let the quiet of the snow engulf me. I felt at peace and knew this was where I was meant to be. Outside, on a well-known trail, but I was exploring just the same. One foot in front of the other, my poles came in handy. I got a rhythm going.

As I broke track, I could feel the snow kick up from the tail of my snowshoe to be caught on the top back edge of my boots. It was cold and the snow would soon be melted on the back of my exercise tights. But it was so quiet and beautiful, I didn't let the wetness bother me. As I walked along, the stillness comforted me. Freed from the stress of work for a few days, being in the mountains with the kids all here, restored my soul and gave me the strength I knew I would need to get through the coming year. I reminded myself to enjoy this walk and let the outdoors cocoon me in its majesty.

I tramped along, foot plants wide so I didn't step on the inside edge of the snowshoe and trip myself. The walking warmed me up and I started to relax as I made good progress toward the log bridge. No trucks passed on the road above me; I had this walk to myself. Or so I thought.

I had almost reached the log bridge, my turning around spot. I paused and pulled out my phone. I took off one glove and tucked that into the pocket of my vest, and used my index finger on the screen of my phone. I took a photo of the bridge; the boys would recognize where I was and be able to anticipate my return to the cabin. The photo was a color shot that captured the late afternoon shadows on the snow. As I took the first photo, I felt a movement to my right, but through the phone lens, I didn't see anything moving.

I lowered the phone and there it was, movement in my right periphery. Then bushy, blondish-black hair that stood straight up. An animal ran behind the log. Maybe it was a dog, but I realized its gait was not that of a dog. It glided along too easily and suddenly, popped up into view. A coyote was on the bridge.

I looked left and right; coyotes could be solitary, but they also run in packs. I didn't see any other animals close by. He hesitated, perfectly balanced in the middle of the log bridge. Quickly, I got my phone back up and snapped another photo. He was beautiful, a majestic animal but a carnivore, probably in search of a small animal along the trail. A young deer, a rabbit, a rodent, or even a fish could have been his next meal.

He hesitated on the bridge, his foreleg stopped mid-step, and pointed back at me. I stared at him and held his gaze. He hesitated. Suddenly, he turned to his right and continued across the log to the other side of the creek, where he jumped down towards the bank and disappeared. I quickly texted the boys my photo, with a message, "I'm on my way back to the cabin." I put my phone back in my pocket and my glove back on as I picked up my poles.

I turned around and that's when I saw his tracks in the snow. The coyote had come up right behind me, then circled back a ways, then ran up and around me behind the fallen trees to get to the bridge. He was not going to be deterred by someone snowshoeing along the creek he wanted to cross. I had no sense he had come up just inches from the back of my snowshoes, nor did I hear him. His tracks in the snow were the only evidence of how close he was to me.

Dear Chris,

I'm not sure I believe in signs, but I still feel your presence often, and in the most natural settings. In this year and a half since your death, a pair of turkeys crossed my path where you took your final run. Three young deer cut across a trail when I was out hiking, a pair of ducks rested easily in a tiny pool in the bend of a creek, and a red fox crossed a trail of dried mule's ears early one morning about twenty feet ahead of me. And today, a coyote hesitated on the bridge to look back at me. Like the full moon every month, the lunar marker of your passing, these animal sightings remind me of the passion you had for the outdoors.

Merry Christmas,
xoxo Sue

Return to the Mountains

THE FOLLOWING YEAR, WE seemed to be better prepared to celebrate the winter holidays with more decorations. We had a new cabin, a cozy, classic A-frame in a mountain community not far from our original cabin. That winter, we decided to decorate the new cabin properly, so the box with the holiday toy soldiers, the stockings, and the reindeer stocking holders made it out of a storage locker and over to the new neighborhood. The familiarity of the decorations, as we unpacked them, seemed to relax us. Besides, there was a new stocking to add to the mantle, a granddaughter had arrived in the fall. She was a welcome and wonderful new addition to our family. With her first smiles and baby giggles, we learned how to laugh again. There was joy and a lightness in our conversations that year; it was time to get Chris's and my stockings out once more. I was able to hang them together as they shared a reindeer stocking holder. For what would our family celebration be without the memory of Chris in our lives?

Due to the car seat configuration now, we returned from our Christmas Eve dinner in town in two cars. The cabin fireplace warmed us all. The foragers in the group discovered the box of See's Candies, sent by a cousin for our holiday sweet fix. Suddenly, the assorted chocolates were passed around and one of the boys' girlfriends was chastised to not pick at the bottom of a piece of candy to discover its inside. We laughed and the sound soothed us all. But as the box made its way around the room, I noticed no one took the corner piece.

The little square piece of brittle, dipped in chocolate and lying in the corner of the box, remained. As it should. It was always the piece Chris picked first, back in the days when my Mom and Dad would arrive at our original cabin, their car full of presents for their young grandsons. After dinner, Mom would make a big deal of passing Chris the See's box so that he got the first pick. She deferred that pick to him, her favorite and only son-in-law, even though she knew he would pick her favorite piece.

At the end of the evening, after reading *The Night Before Christmas* and *The Polar Express* to the baby, we stretched out on the couches and finished up conversations before we headed for bed. I turned down the gas fireplace and began tidying up the living room just a bit. People magazines in one pile, miscellaneous devices charging on the kitchen island, and the top back on the box of See's Candies. I noticed the corner piece remained.

Chris's absence hit me once again as I tried to focus on the positive. Ah yes, the corner piece reminded me of all our past Christmases, full of life and energy and his party spirits. But I hoped someone new would sneak the corner piece tomorrow, maybe even for breakfast, and a new tradition would emerge for our family.

With the promise of the holiday beginning in a new cabin and of candlelight reflecting on a new baby's face, the glow and wonder of all things possible returned to our family's midwinter celebration. For there, on the far-left edge of the mantle, hung both Chris's and my stockings together once again.

After New Year's, the kids returned to their homes, and I took down the mantle decorations. I returned the stockings to the box and put the box away in the garage, remembering to be thankful for all the holidays we did share with Chris.

Next year will be easier, I promised myself.

I continued to realize that many decisions I faced in creating a new future would be mine alone to make. But Christmas belongs to our sons, their wives, and their families as well. The past will fuse with the future, and together we will celebrate both the bittersweet and the joys in the holiday seasons to come.

Crossing

I ARRIVED AT THE turnout early. I wanted to do this hike before the mountain bikers, runners, and dogs got out on the trail. I looked forward to the solitude. My experience as a widow has been not just one of isolation, but also of choices; I could choose loneliness or solitude. I chose the latter; it was my way of diving deeper into my feelings to make peace with this new way of living on my own.

I parked the car and sat still for a few moments. In the early morning stillness, I heard a truck downshifting out on the highway, the birds awakening, and the creek gurgled. It was running now, not roaring as it was earlier this year at the start of springtime. I got out of the car, retied my day hikers and retrieved the poles from the hatchback. I slipped off my lightweight puffer jacket and stowed it in the back of the car. I wouldn't need it; the sky was blue and there was not a breath of wind in the trees that morning. I threw on my daypack. It was lighter than the packs I used to carry, yet it had the essentials—a water bottle, some snacks, a trail map, a Swiss Army knife, a small first aid kit, a ChapStick. My phone was in my back pocket, a digital compass just a tap away. The more I have hiked, the less I've carried. I fiddled with the straps, grabbed my poles and headed out. My routines as a solo hiker were becoming predictable, ones that I could execute without too much thinking. But that day felt different.

The trail was a familiar one—the same one Chris and I hiked and snowshoed before we had the boys, the same one where we would bring the boys to try and find the beaver dam, the same one where I saw a coyote on the old log bridge that second Christmas after Chris passed away. This was the same trail where I snowshoed alone that first Valentine's Day after his death, where I used my ski pole and carved a big heart in a snowbank, encircling both of our initials.

The trail was dry but not yet summer-dusty. The visitors to this region hadn't arrived yet. I paused and breathed in and felt the morning sun start to warm me up. My shoulders pulled back, balancing the daypack, and I set out at an easy walking pace. As if an endorphin clicked in my brain, I suddenly felt peaceful, happy even, as I picked my way around the small rocks on the trail. The sound of the creek reassured me. As my body warmed up, my creaky arthritic joints started to stretch out a bit. The walking became easier, my stride a little longer, and I fell into a steady pace—not the rushed pace to get to a destination, but just steady.

There would be no bushwhacking that day. Those days were behind me, belonging to a time when Chris needed to forge a new trail whenever we headed out into the wilderness. Without him, today was just an easy hike on a well-traveled and familiar trail to a bend in the creek where I would sit and reflect.

I thought I needed to carry the burden of my grief with me forever to not forget Chris. Much of that burden had become more manageable, my daypack lighter. Time had softened some of the rough edges of my initial grief and I could hike and enjoy the experience, even when I was by myself.

I sank into a peaceful state of acceptance. I breathed in the fresh air. It felt chilly on my cheeks, yet refreshing. I settled into my hiking pace and anticipated stepping over or around the rocks and roots on the trail. A sense of knowing this trail calmed me and provided comfort as I walked. An hour, then part of a second hour, slipped by.

When I reached my stopping place, the heavy snow of last winter had moved some of the rocks around. But I found a level one, set my poles next to it and eased myself down. The rock felt chilly on my bum. I shook my daypack off and opened it up, retrieving my water bottle and an energy bar. The sound of the creek soothed me. I heard a bird in the distance, but otherwise, the trail was quiet that morning. It was still early.

I couldn't begin to recall the number of times we did this hike together. My widow brain couldn't recall a number, but I could remember the familiarity of this place and the laughter and joy we shared walking it. That morning, I tried to reflect on gratitude. I was thankful for two grandchildren. When I heard our oldest son speak to his daughters, sometimes my breath caught in my throat. The words echoed what his father said to him as a child, only they were repeated in his own adult voice. As the years passed and the lump in my throat slowly got smaller, I could be thankful for the shared life I had with Chris, while still missing him and with a twinge of sadness that he could not be here with me to share and enjoy the life I got to keep living.

That day I was also relieved and comforted to know I had not forgotten him. Sometimes, I would get a fleeting notion that his presence was close to me, like the time late last summer when a red fox cut across my path only four to five feet away. He might have been just under a year old, long, sleek body, his tail almost straight out; he looked like he was hunting in the early morning. He didn't seem to notice that I was even on the trail. Red foxes are known to mate for life and I wondered if that was a sign from Chris. Continue to live your life as you must, but know I will always be close.

As I rested on the rock, I noticed the grove of pine trees that surrounded me. It was windy. Back and forth they bent, their

71

tops swaying. The sky was clear and the sun shone through the grove, but the wind challenged the trees to withstand its power. If I listened carefully, I could almost hear the creak of the trunks as they gave in to the wind but did not break.

Up the canyon a way, I spotted it. One of the trees must have been struck by lightning last year. The dead tree was downed. Getting up from the rock, I walked up closer to it. I could see where the lightning struck. A black streak, looking like charcoal, ran along part of the trunk. I could only imagine how the tree fell. There would have been a flash of lightning, a thunderous cracking sound—chemical, light, heat—striking the tallest tree and topping it powerfully. The sound in the forest would have been deafening. The stricken tree went down, almost to the forest floor, and took with it some of the branches from the neighboring trees. It did not catch fire. Instead, it looked like it smoldered, died and became downed lumber, uprooted from its life source of soil and water.

I walked closer, and in the dirt and dust at the tree's base, I noticed a seedling. The surrounding trees showed signs of new growth in their peripheral needles. They had more light for their own photosynthesis now. The older tree, that was so big and so strong, had cast a wide shadow over the others, slowing their own growth. Months after the strike, the surrounding trees showed signs of new green needles at the tips of their branches, which were spreading wider.

I couldn't help but think of Chris and the impact he had on our lives. He was the tallest tree in our little forest, and as much as he was the center of our family, his shadow cast a wide protective shield over us that was now gone. We were the understory trees, content to be in his shade, twisting our branches and needles for the sunlight we needed. But now, the sunlight was shining on the saplings. Out of the shadows, our sons and daughters-in-law were growing and reaching towards their own stars as well, in their own family stands.

I walked back to sit on the rock perch. I lost track of time.

A rustle in the bushes behind me interrupted my musings. I twisted around to see a deer had come down the hillside behind me in search of fresh leaves on the bushes. She paused, then continued to nibble on the bush. I finished my snack, my thinking time over. I got up, stretched my legs, and put my daypack back on. I picked up my poles. A dog barked in the distance and the deer scampered up, away from the trail. The sun was higher in the sky now; the trail would get busier. I heard a bicycle coming up behind me and stepped aside to let the rider pass.

I hiked back towards the car. The solitude of that morning hike in the mountains restored my spirit. I knew I couldn't live in my memory zone forever. My grief had enveloped me in a holding pattern, and yet I sensed the time was getting closer for me to move forward and create a new phase of my life.

I imagined it would always be like this. As I moved forward and learned to appreciate the joys of life still to come, I would also learn to live with the moments of loss and sadness that crept in like a small, loose rock from the trail that somehow found its way into my shoe.

I arrived back at the bridge, stopped in the middle, and stared up the wash towards the creek's source. The sound of the water cascading around the rocks calmed me. Nature felt restorative. I did not know if I would pass this way again. I crossed the bridge and headed home.

Chris in Squaw Valley

Pt. Reyes trailhead, last hike

CBW Rest in Peace

Our next generation of hikers

The Scout

I HAVE FINALLY REALIZED that Chris rests in peace, along with both sets of our parents. Looking back, I sometimes wondered how much Chris's adventurous spirit attracted me to him. He lived outside my comfort level and challenged me. So many times, I learned I could do what I didn't think was possible. Traversing along a ridgeline with sheer drops on either side was simultaneously nerve-racking and exhilarating. As I looked downhill, I would have preferred to be hiking across the meadow. Yet, my life with him was always a new adventure. Would I have been happy with a mate who was more predictable in his behavior, maybe making safer choices to stay on the trail instead of cutting cross country? Maybe. But Chris was never boring, he always had a different way of approaching a goal and proposing a solution: "We'll just make our own trail, we'll be fine." Even to this day, his confident words continue to echo in my brain and my heart.

Years into our marriage, I thought he was born in the wrong era. Chris would have thrived as a scout on horseback in the Lewis and Clark expeditions; he could ride, shoot a rifle, and draw a map. As an explorer, he would have been on his own timetable. He tried working as an accountant after college, and, despite doing well and having advancement opportunities presented to him, he chose to leave the safety of those types of jobs to pursue his entrepreneurial spirit. His internal drive was set to live life outside the safety of boundaries set by others. He really lived life on his own terms.

Early on, I realized trying to reign him in would have created upheavals for our family. Instead, I created a path for me to follow, with organized schedules and routines, as I willingly supported his exploring ways.

I have discovered simpler joys in my life now and choices that are risk averse. During COVID-19, I stayed connected with family and friends through technology; Zoom and FaceTime calls replaced the coffee catchups with colleagues from a life phase that seems so long ago. Recently retired, the time constraints of raising kids and pursuing a career are behind me. There are more opportunities for candid conversations with both old and new friends, for sharing life experiences and discussions on more meaningful levels. Maybe this change in perspective comes with age, but for me, it also came with accepting my grief.

I miss Chris, of course. I miss the spontaneity, the challenge, the energized conversations that came with discussing the bushwhacking way. Together, we would be trying something new and unexplored, leaving behind the comfort and safety that came with established routines like following the trail. We would discuss the grade and condition of the new route, the amount of brush we might encounter, how much daylight was left in the afternoon. Maybe part of my aging process has been to settle into established and comfortable routines; the same toasted muffin, fruit, and coffee every morning doesn't necessitate a lot of thought. Breakfast just happens. Yet his death left a huge void in my life, and in some ways dulled my own sense of wanting more risky explorations that test my limits. I miss being part of a team; our conversations and working together towards a shared or common goal pleased me. Now, I calculate risks before I act. I am the solitary skier on the more populated and groomed runs, the solo hiker with poles and a map on a well-traveled trail.

I miss the chaotic start to the day with him, throwing on clothes and hiking boots, grabbing a jacket, a daypack, and a water bottle, skipping breakfast to pick up a coffee and a muffin on the way to explore some new town, park, or trail. As the surviving parent, I do these activities in a more calculated and, yes, probably safer way now. My hiking trail can be long and strenuous, but it is well marked. After a long day of following traverses and cairns along the way, it is satisfying enough for me to reach the overlook where other hikers before me have enjoyed the view.

When I see our sons, I recognize flashes of their father in their manners of speaking, the jokes they tell, the books they read, and the interests they pursue. Grown into adults now, two with wives and children of their own, I envision a future for them of their own friend and family holidays, professional pursuits, children, and cousin adventures at the cabin. I sense my work as a parent is almost finished. Hopefully, my recovery from a devastating event and displays of perseverance and resilience to build a new life will inspire and comfort them when I, too, am gone. Between their father's enthusiasm for life and my own inner drive, I sense they will have the strength to forge their own life paths.

A grandchild begins kindergarten, and her little sister starts preschool. A grandson is born and blessed with the middle name Christopher. A new grandson arrives, and is loved by his big brother and his cousins. Their lives reinforce my peace of knowing cycles of life continue, regardless of the damage my scarred heart has experienced along the way. Rocking my new grandson to sleep, I hold him close and whisper one of his grandpa's secrets of living: *Keep exploring.*

Epilogue: Gathering Up a Child

I CUT ACROSS THE teachers' parking lot and waited for my granddaughter in the shade of an old elm tree. In the glare of the afternoon sun, the dusky shade cooled off the grassy area, and provided a respite for me and the rest of the parents, grandparents, nannies and friends collecting our children.

In the gaggle of transitional kindergarteners, I heard her before I spotted her. Her voice, loud and determined, shouted an alert—the boys are getting closer! The girls darted around the play yard and squealed as the boys closed in, trying to tag them. The chasing became more chaotic, like same pole magnets repelling each other. Suddenly, I saw her come to an abrupt stop. She was energetically waving at me, trying to get my attention.

"Susu, Susu, I'm over here."

I gave her a quick wave back and she returned to the chasing game. Glancing at my watch, I saw there were still five minutes left in recess before the school day ended.

The bell rang and the children lined up behind each other. The boys and girls each jockeyed for positions near the front of the line. The teacher stood at the gate and checked her watch. Like worms trying to shimmy out of a jar, the children stretched their sweaty necks and leaned around the back of their classmates' heads to see who was picking them up that day.

My granddaughter was excited to leave school early. I watched her whisper in a playmate's ear and point to me to say that her grandma was picking her up. The teacher dismissed each student one by one and greeted each of us picking up our little ones. Identifications were unnecessary; the children's hugs confirmed who belonged to whom. I was reassured to see that my grandchild is part of this neighborhood school community.

As I bent down for a hug, my granddaughter quickly twirled around and shed her backpack for me to carry. We clasped hands. Crossing the street, we jaywalked towards my car. Opening the back door, I motioned for her to climb up into the car seat. She was too heavy for me to be able to lift her into it. As she turned around and settled, looking forward, her legs splayed outwards. I tried to pull the straps down around her shoulders. She squealed. They were pinching her. I thought I had just lengthened these a few weeks ago, but she was growing so fast now. She was too big for this seat and the next-generation high-backed booster seat had been on back-order. In addition to her physical growth, her vocabulary had exploded. She had even started to read *Dory Fantasmagory* books aloud. I wondered if my afternoons of reading to her were waning. Soon our roles would start to shift. She will be the one reading *The Polar Express* to me on our winter holiday nights when we cuddle in front of our cabin fireplace.

Finally, she was buckled in, and we headed for the frozen yogurt shop for an after-school treat. Looking out the window, she recognized the route we were taking and announced what flavor her little sister would like. It was a purple raspberry dairy-free concoction that we brought home and popped into the freezer. After dinner, Sissy would be surprised with her treat.

Then, like two bear cubs, we nestled in, sitting at the kitchen table. We giggled as we enjoyed trading bites with each other's Fro-yo flavors and began planning the rest of the afternoon. Wiggling out of her seat, she ran to the playroom and returned with the small magnifying glass I gave her over the holidays last year. That afternoon, we would play "explorer."

We left her house for a neighborhood walk. A few doors down, we stopped at a neighbor's house with two turtle statues in the front garden. We squatted down on our haunches. She held the magnifying glass close to the ground and looked for roly-poly bugs in the shredded bark. We didn't spot any, so we stood up and continued our exploration.

We headed over to the cul-de-sac where a grassy area was ringed with rocks, rose bushes, and some tall hedges along the fence lines. The grass was damp, even in the late afternoon sun, and some of the rocks were wet. Bending down, I turned one over. A burst of ants scurried around every which way. My granddaughter knelt, getting her magnifying glass so close to the ants she almost touched them. They were too fast to count, but under the rock, she also spotted two earwigs. She pointed out their long, black, skinny bodies with pinchers on their "butts." We both laughed. She also found the tiniest red spider on the sidewalk, so tiny I saw it only when it moved.

Gradually, we turned the rocks back over. We rubbed our dirty hands together, shaking off some of the damp dirt. The half-moons of dirt under our nails reminded me of my late husband's love of puttering in our old backyard, when he tended to his roses. His sudden death left a gap in each of our lives. In the spring, when his favorite Sally Holmes climbers started to bloom, my grief bubbled to the surface. I remembered a time of homegrown bouquets on the kitchen table, sharing a glass of wine and a beer at the end of the day on the deck overlooking the garden. But that time has come and gone.

Turning so slightly, my granddaughter easily offered her hand up towards mine. Her small, soft hand, slightly balled up, comfortably fit into my wrinkly and bony hand. When I wrapped my hand around her chubby one, all I wanted to do was to protect her. It was the softness and innocence of her touch that united us and made me want to shield her from anything traumatic that life may hold for her future. We circled the grassy area and headed back to her home, still holding hands.

Suddenly, she looked up and asked, "Susu, do you want to get married?"

Caught off-guard, I answered vaguely. "Well. Maybe. That's a sweet idea."

"Susu, if you got married, Daddy would have a dad."

My gut clenched. Of course, finally I got it. Even a child can understand the empty seat at the dinner table and how missing him affected each one of us in our family pod. Kneeling, I gathered her in my arms and pulled her close. My hug was full of hope for her future, her family's future, and for my own future as well. Whispering in her ear, my voice wobbled. "Yes, little one, if I get married, your Daddy will have a dad."

I stood up and turned away, not wanting her to see the solitary tear behind my sunglasses. We joined hands and walked home.

Acknowledgements

My writing explores a time after Chris's death when I realized he no longer belonged only to me. Instead, his death created a community of family and friends, many of them also grieving, who became my family's support team. I owe thanks to many people who continue to keep their own stories of adventures with Chris alive in our hearts.

First, to my editor, Karen "Kat" Terrey, tangledrootswriting.com. This memoir could not have been possible without your support and encouragement. Your willingness to work with a new and aspiring writer continues to be a fulfilling learning experience for me. I appreciate your kindness and consistency in teaching me how to write sentences that can tell a story.

A special acknowledgment and thanks to graphic designer Jacqueline Gilman, jgilmandesign.com, who created the cover and interior design. She works the magic of turning a manuscript into a book.

Thank you, D.D. van Löben Sels, princesstiger.com, for designing the bookmark. Chris couldn't have had a better birthday buddy.

To the early readers Peg Casselberry, Linda Schacht Gage, Chela Richheimer, and our sons, thank you for sharing your insights. They are appreciated.

To Janet Saalfeld, Rob Pomeroy, Michael Machette, Fred Nachtwey, James Nachtwey, Rick Woodward, and our sons, Alex Woodward, James Woodward, and Drew Woodward, thank you for sharing your stories at Chris's memorial. Your reminiscences about bushwhacking, skiing, coaching Little League, errant golf shots, and his favorite New Yorker cartoons captured Chris's personality as we celebrated his life.

To Rob and Sue Pomeroy, Lindsay Lloyd, Bob Book

(Padre Peregrino), Dick Saalfeld, the Jims in my life, Jim Smith, Jim Richman and Jim Nebel, Chip and Mary Brown, Page van Löben Sels, Warren Davis, John Gage, David Good, Geordie Bassett, Rick Mayer, Glenn Rogers, Vince Saunders, Steve Brown, Steve Casselberry, Chris Forehan, Panos Papadopoulos, Brad and Debbie Boer, Bruce and Bev Feder, I say thank you. Your collective willingness to stay connected with our family, whether camping at the Lair, attending Cal events, golfing, hiking, tailgating, swimming laps, or sharing a meal, has helped my family continue to find joy in our lives.

To Robin Machette, Ruth Donohugh, Linda Schacht Gage, Nancy Zacher, Peg Casselberry, Diana Duey, Janet Saalfeld, Janet Richman, Sharon Smith, Penny Lloyd, D.D. van Löben Sels, Claire Nicholson, Toni Farb, Andrea Campos, Sandy Rogin, Holly Tigard, Helen Marcus, Jeanne Huang Li, Jeanette Duff, and Julie Nachtwey, I owe thanks. As my "sisters-in-spirit" the adventures and stories we continue to share strengthen our bonds.

A special acknowledgement to my late parents, Toots and Pops, for their love, guidance, and support for both Chris and me. During a time of deep sorrow, I expressed to Pops the frustration at the bureaucracy in settling Chris's affairs. He looked at me, paused, and said, "Don't be so hard on yourself." His words continue to comfort me. Thanks, Pops.

And to my family, Rick Woodward, Margot Woodward, Judi Woodward Archbold, Robin Nenninger Nugent, Bob Nugent, Todd Johnson, Brad Johnson, my nieces and nephews, and Alex Woodward, Elana Woodward, James Woodward, Drew Woodward, Emily Woodward and the grandchildren, I say thank you. The way each of you keeps a special memory of Chris close to your heart continues to inspire me. I am grateful to be surrounded by family love.

With gratitude to all.

Author's Note

THIS MEMOIR BEGAN AS some stories I wrote to share with our sons. After Chris's sudden death, I wanted the boys to have a sense of Chris's and my early life together, before we became a family. Over time, the manuscript evolved into a broader story of our family's love of the outdoors, a devastating loss, and the healing power of nature.

This work is based on my journals, recollections, maps, and police and coroner reports. Some names and locations have been changed to protect the privacy of individuals. The dialogue has been recreated from my journals and memory. The football story is a compilation of remembrances from attending games with Chris when I moved to Berkeley in the Fall of 1973.

About the Author

Susan Woodward developed her passion for outdoor sports and writing as a student-athlete at the University of California, Berkeley. After graduating, she coached tennis at Mills College for six seasons before returning to Berkeley where she was the lone woman working in the Press Box on football game days. She wrote the radio drops, corporate sponsor ad copy and public affairs announcements for the network radio broadcasters and the stadium public address announcer. Later in her career, she worked in development and wrote gift proposals, donor correspondences and talking points for various deans.

In forty years of marriage, she and her late husband, Chris, hiked on six continents. They missed Antarctica. A seasonal resident in the Sierra since 1981, and recently retired, she volunteers as a hiking docent for the Truckee Donner Land Trust, and hosts "Susu's Nature Camp" for her grandchildren. When she's not writing, she can often be found out on the trails, accompanied by her sons and their families.

What Happens When Your Heart Breaks?